# Granted!

Linda F. Radke, President
Five Star Publications, Inc.
PO Box 6698
Chandler, AZ 85246-6698
480-940-8182

www.CafeGranted.com

Five Star Publications, Inc.
*Your Story Begins Here*
Since 1985

Library of Congress Cataloging-in-Publication Data

Taylor, Chris.
  Granted! : a teacher's guide to writing & winning classroom grants / by Chris Taylor.
     p. cm.
  ISBN-13: 978-1-58985-113-9
  ISBN-10: 1-58985-113-7
  1. Educational fund raising--United States--Handbooks, manuals, etc. 2. Proposal writing for grants--United States--Handbooks, manuals, etc. 3. Education--United States--Finance--Handbooks, manuals, etc. I. Title.
  LC243.T39 2009
  371.2'06--dc22
                        2009012155

Printed in the United States of America

Cover Design by Kris Taft
Interior Design by Linda Longmire
Project Manager: Sue DeFabis

First Edition

10 9 8 7 6 5 4 3 2 1

# Table of Contents

4

*Dedicated to:*

My First Teacher

My Mother

Rose Taylor

6

Granted!

# Welcome to your journey to write and win grants to support learning in your classroom!

"Learning and teaching should not stand on opposite banks and just watch the river flow by; instead, they should embark together on a journey down the water." These words of educator Loris Malaguzzi ring true every time teachers' efforts to teach and students' desire to learn mesh. The results are powerful and rewarding for both teachers and students.

As a teacher, you probably have many ideas for projects that would assist your efforts to teach and, in turn, enhance your students' desire to learn. However, lack of funding may have stopped you from being able to implement these innovations in your classroom. Learning and teaching remain "on opposite banks" without ever having the opportunity to begin a "journey" together.

*Granted! A Teacher's Guide to Writing & Winning Classroom Grants* offers you the tools to make that journey happen. It helps to make your innovative project of enhanced teaching and learning a reality through an award of grant funding.

Follow the process set forth in *Granted!,* and you will be on your way to writing and winning grants to fund classroom projects.

Welcome to the journey!

Granted!

# Granted!

## A Teacher's
## GUIDE
### to Writing & Winning
### Classroom Grants

Chris
**TAYLOR**

2009

Granted!

# CHAPTER ONE:
## The Grant Process

Granted!

# So Many Ideas, So Little Money:
## The Need for Non-traditional Methods of Funding for Teachers' Classroom Projects

The ancient philosopher Epicretus once wrote, "Only the educated are free." That statement may be true. Perhaps only the educated are free, but education certainly isn't! According to the U.S. Department of Education, taxpayers in the United States invested about $536 billion in kindergarten through 12th-grade education for the 2004-2005 school year. Yet, with all the money spent on schools, per student spending and the amount spent within the classroom are actually decreasing. The federal government provides 8.3% of education funding, and private sources provide 8.9%. The rest of the money for education comes from state and local governments. Although that amount of revenue for fiscal year 2006 amounted to $473.1 billion, that funding could be shrinking in your state.

The present state of the economy has impacted the amount of funding states can provide their K-12 education. In 2008, Ron Snell of the National Conference of State Legislatures reflected on this situation when he said, "K-12 education is nearly sacrosanct in state finance. It is the biggest item of expenditure in every state. Even so…states are cutting K-12 education." Many states are experiencing such cuts. The Center on Budget and Policy Priorities studies programs and policies that affect low- and moderate-income families and individuals, including education. A February 2009 report of the organization stated, "Thirty-six states have cut education or proposed such cuts because they face massive, devastating budget deficits in this recession."

The Rockefeller Institute studies education funding. In a 2007 report, it stated that since 2002, the amount of real spending by state and local governments for each student has decreased. This decrease was particularly true for states that are traditionally low education spenders. In addition, in the last three years, the amount of money the president has budgeted for the U.S. Department of Education has decreased. This has impacted rural schools especially hard.

Regardless of whether you teach in a lower spending state or in a rural area, as a teacher you witness problems relating to school funding every day. You see firsthand the needs in your classroom that aren't being met. You understand your students would benefit from books and supplies that simply aren't available. You know more equipment and computers would go a long way to help your students. You envision the learning opportunities that would be presented by classroom visits from authors, artists and other professionals. So, you often use your own money to provide what is needed for your students that can't be funded through traditional means.

As the amount of per pupil education funding falls, the more money teachers, like you, spend from their own pockets. Horace Mann, an early education leader, said, "Teachers teach because they care. Teaching young people is what they do best. It requires long hours, patience and care." However, teaching now seems to also require money from the teacher's own pocket to supplement the costs of education within the classroom. Yet, teachers remain the "caring" individuals that Horace Mann described. This caring is clearly shown not only by the fact that teachers spend their own money to help their students, but also by the fact that these out-of-pocket expenditures by teachers for classroom materials and supplies have steadily increased.

A survey from a few years ago by the National School Supply and Equipment Association estimated teachers' classroom spending to be an average of $589 a year for school supplies and instruction materials. Fifty-six percent of teachers surveyed said they used their own money for instructional materials, and 75% paid for school supplies for their classrooms from their own money. The American Federation of Teachers says, "Teachers as a group spend more than $1.3 billion of their personal funds on classroom materials per year—and that's based on the more conservative $437 per-teacher average of two years ago."

Realistically, teachers can't be expected to fill the funding gap between actual funding and needed funding. So, many projects and programs they would like to offer their students go unfunded, and classroom learning suffers. Teachers have so many good ideas, but so little money to make those ideas become reality.

At the same time that teachers are spending more in their classrooms out of their own money, they are being required to expand their curriculum in order to meet educational standards established by various governmental entities. These standards are often in the form of mandates and appear to be increasing at the same time funding in the classroom seems to be decreasing. These standards are often difficult to meet at best,

Granted!

and at worst are impossible to meet without additional classroom assistance.

Under such circumstances, teaching grows more difficult. Writer and educator Fawn M. Brodie said, "Housework is a breeze. Cooking is a pleasant diversion. Putting up a retaining wall is a lark. But teaching is like climbing a mountain." The effort of teachers to meet educational standards within a system that has little funding available for innovative programs and projects to support those standards must indeed feel, at times, like climbing a mountain! But, there are ways to make that mountain seem more like a hill. Nontraditional funding sources are available to help teachers develop and implement projects and programs to support the meeting of educational standards within their classrooms. These funding sources are the public and private entities that offer the opportunity for teachers to receive money to help their students through the award of a grant.

# What Is a Grant? Who Gives Them? Who Gets Them?

**Definition:** *Webster's New Universal Unabridged Dictionary defines the verb "grant" as "to bestow or confer," while the noun "grant" means something has been granted such as "a sum of money." Thus, a grant involves the giving of money. With regard to teachers needing additional classroom funds, a grant is an award of money from a nontraditional source to assist in fulfilling those needs.*

## ■ Grants: *Available Funds*

There are different types of grants that expand the dictionary definition of a "grant." Various grant awarding entities may define what a grant is according to their own guidelines. For example, the federal government awards many grants each year. It provides the following definition for grants in the website it devotes to its grant process, www.grants.gov. "Grants are not Benefits or Entitlements. A federal Grant is an award of financial assistance from a federal agency to a recipient to carry out a public purpose of support or stimulation authorized by a law of the United States. Grants are not federal assistance or loans to individuals."

Note that the federal government definition expands on the simple idea of a grant as just being an award of money. It includes the purpose for which the money is to be spent and makes it clear the award is final and not simply a loan.

Many grant entities are corporations. Microsoft is a corporation that gives many grants each year. Microsoft sets out its definition of a grant on its website, www.microsoft.com. A grant is defined by Microsoft as a: "…sum of money that is given to your business after an application process has been followed. There is no interest to be paid and funds awarded do not usually have to be repaid - as long as the terms of the grant are met."

This definition focuses on the fact that the money given through a grant is part of an entire process established by the grant giving entity that must be followed. It makes clear that in order to win a grant one must study the guidelines and procedures of the particular grant awarding entity.

Grants may be given by many different entities to support many different causes. The United Nations makes grants to developing countries to create programs dealing with global environmental issues. The federal government provides grants to arts organizations through the National Endowment of the Arts. The Bill and Melinda Gates Foundation offers grants to support efforts by nonprofit groups to eradicate diseases. Many entities award grants to assist educational pursuits at every level.

The federal government offers education grants in many different forms. Examples of these government grants show the wide range of activities they fund. The federal government gives need-based grants directly to low-income college students. It provides block grants to state departments of education to pursue a variety of programs. Many federal agencies offer grants to support educational projects, such as the Department of Labor's grant programs to help troubled youth.

States also have grants that support education. For example, the Iowa Department of Education issues grants to school districts for its Reading First Program, and the Hawaii State Foundation on Culture and the Arts offers arts education grants. Many local governments give education grants as well. Numerous school districts or their education foundations have grants that support teachers and schools.

In addition to government sources, grants may be awarded by corporations, foundations, nonprofit entities and even individuals. Some examples of those grants include Starbucks' grants that support literacy, the Spencer Foundation's research grants that study education in America and abroad, the United Way's funding of mini-grants for teachers to support classroom projects or informal gifts by everyday people to support

Granted!

education in their local communities.

Grants that promote education range from those awarding millions of dollars from the federal government to a state department of education to those providing mini-grants of $100 each made by a local business to deserving teachers. No matter the form, money is available from nontraditional sources to support education, and these funds can help create and implement projects and programs that will go a long way toward promoting learning in the classroom. Help exists for teachers to enhance the education of their students. Grants are available. Teachers just need some information and guidance to make their wishes for their students *"Granted!"*

## ■ Givers: *Grant Awarding Entities*

Grants are only one way people and organizations give to causes important to them. In fact, the Giving Institute, formerly the American Association of Fundraising Counsel, studied America's philanthropy and found that Americans gave close to $300 billion for various causes, both religious and secular, in 2006. This amount was a 4.2% increase from the year before. But, most of this money didn't come from businesses. Seventy-six percent of charitable giving was contributed by individuals or households. Foundations increased their giving, which amounted to 12.4% of all philanthropy, while corporate giving declined to 4.2%. Of this giving, $41 billion or 13.9% of total philanthropy went for education. These large sums of money are given through all kinds of philanthropy, not just money awarded by grants.

### GOVERNMENT

In addition to funding by private sources, government at all levels gives millions of dollars each year to support programs that will benefit the public in some way. In fact, the 2007 annual report of the Federal Assistance Award Data System stated that 26 agencies issued grants for over $13 million just through the federal grants website, www.grants.gov. In fact, the federal government spent $460 billion or 14% of total expenditures on grants in fiscal year 2004. Of course, much of this money goes to state and local governments who must administer federally mandated programs. But, these state and local governments also award millions of dollars in grants each year. These statistics indicate one of the primary "givers" of grants is the government.

# FOUNDATIONS

Foundations are also "givers" of grant funding. These entities may be public or private in nature. The Foundation Center, an authoritative information source on philanthropy, defines a foundation as: "an entity that is established as a nonprofit corporation or a charitable trust, with a principal purpose of making grants to unrelated organizations or institutions or to individuals for scientific, educational, cultural, religious or other charitable purposes."

A private foundation's funds usually come from a single individual, family or corporation. For example, Target Corporation has a foundation that offers grants, as does the Doris Duke Charitable Foundation. A public foundation gets its funding from several sources which may include individuals, groups, governments, private foundations and even fees. Some school districts, such as the Deer Valley Unified School District in Arizona, have foundations that award grants to teachers and schools within their districts. Many communities organize foundations to support various causes within their jurisdictions, such as the Community Foundation of Middle Tennessee.

The Foundation Center tracks the giving of grants of $10,000 or more by the largest foundations that were not given to individuals. Further, certain community foundation grants were also not included. The Center found that in 2005 the number of foundations it tracked was 1,154. These foundations gave 130,961 grants representing over $16 billion.

# CORPORATIONS

Many for-profit and nonprofit corporations offer grants. Some may have formed foundations as the grant-giving arm of their corporation. Others may give grants directly through the corporation. The National Philanthropic Trust reported that 2006 corporate giving, including grants through corporate foundations, amounted to $13.8 billion. Examples of corporate giving include the Teacher Partnership Program of Wells Fargo Bank and the American Legion's grants to disabled veterans.

## ASSOCIATIONS

The term "association" may refer to a variety of different groups. The American Society of Association Executives explains that an association may represent a profession or it may be a trade association composed of business competitors. There are also philanthropic and charitable associations. Many associations award grants. For example, the National Gardening Association works with sponsoring companies and organizations to award grants for projects that involve children in gardening and improve the quality of life for their communities. The American Heart Association funds research grants to scientists. The University of New Hampshire Parents Association gives grants for projects that positively impact the university community. Another related legal entity is the charitable trust. An example of such trusts is the Pew Charitable Trust that partners with donors, public and private organizations and individuals to fund programs designed to improve society.

## RELIGIOUS ORGANIZATIONS

Churches and religious organizations give money to many individuals and groups that support their religious causes. In addition, charitable trusts, foundations, corporations and individuals may provide grant money for religious purposes. Some examples include grants for programs to help intellectually challenged adults by the Knights of Columbus, a Catholic men's group, and grants to various anti-hunger programs by MAZON, a collective entity of about 900 synagogues and over 100,000 individuals.

## SMALL BUSINESSES AND INDIVIDUALS

In addition to the myriad of governmental entities, corporations, associations, trusts and religious groups that provide funding to worthwhile causes, many small businesses and individuals help in both large and small ways. A toy store may donate Christmas gifts to a local children's hospital or a real estate office may give a neighborhood high school money to send the girls' basketball team to a tournament. A retired newspaper reporter may pay copying costs so his grandson's school paper can publish its first edition. These generous efforts may be less complicated than the process to receive a grant from a large entity, but they are still the bestowing of money on another for a charitable purpose, so they may be considered as informal grants.

# ■ Getters: *Entities Qualified to Receive Grants*

Many different types of entities can be grant givers. But, who can receive grants? Who are the grant "getters?" Similar to grant givers, there are many types of grant getters.

## 1. Organizations and Individuals Pursuant to the Grant Document

Who qualifies to receive a grant depends on the guidelines and requirements of each grant. Thus, it is important to check the grant entity's application and related documents to see who may request consideration to receive its grant. A discussion in Chapter Four will help you discover where to find information about grant entities and their grant processes. A quick review of this data shows exactly who can apply for that entity's grant.

Some grants may be from one governmental entity to another, such as grants from the federal to a state government. They may be from individual to individual, as grants made from everyday people to low income college students. They could be from a for-profit corporation to a nonprofit corporation. There are lots of possibilities. One example of possible "getters" of grants is the nonprofit corporation; another is an educational institution.

## 2. Example: 501(c)(3) Nonprofit Corporations

Many grant entities only award grants to groups that support some public interest like public schools or nonprofit corporations. Nonprofit corporations are organized under section 501(c)(3) of federal Internal Revenue Service statutes. The IRS defines 501(c)(3) organizations as those that are organized and operated exclusively for specific purposes listed in the law as: "…charitable, religious, educational, scientific, literary, testing for public safety, fostering national or international amateur sports competition, and preventing cruelty to children or animals. The term *charitable* is used in its generally accepted legal sense and includes relief of the poor, the distressed or the underprivileged; advancement of religion; advancement of education or science; erecting or maintaining public buildings, monuments or works; lessening the burdens of government; lessening neighborhood tensions; eliminating prejudice and discrimination; defending human and civil rights secured by law; and combating community deterioration and juvenile delinquency."
The earnings of a nonprofit can't benefit any private shareholder, individual or private interests, and it can't be

involved in political and legislative activities. It is eligible to receive tax deductible contributions.

Many nonprofits are grant "getters." For example, a community theater group organized as a nonprofit corporation may receive a grant from the state's arts commission. A nonprofit group that helps immigrants may be helped with operating expenses through a grant from a private foundation. A nonprofit research institute may win a grant from the federal government to develop a program to study health care information.

## ■ Givers, Getters and Teachers

You can see from this review of information about grants that funds are available to help teachers with projects to support classroom learning. Grant "givers" often focus on educational causes when awarding grants. The "getters" of such grants are often educators and educational institutions. You are a teacher with lots of great ideas to improve learning in your classroom. Now you can become a grant "getter" by seeking and winning funding for your project ideas from a grant "giver."

## 1. Givers

Grant entities offer billions of dollars each year for education. A large part of this money is the over $34 billion the federal government gives to states for education. But, lesser amounts are also available for educational pursuits. All of the categories of grant givers described above are sources of funding teachers and schools may rely on to support a variety of education projects at the local school level.

Many examples of entities that give education-related grants may be presented. "Teaching Tolerance," a project of the Southern Poverty Law Center, gives grants for up to $10,000 to schools and school districts for programs that bring educators, researchers, parents and students together to equalize students' experiences in schools, such as projects to advocate for special education or to reduce prejudice in racially isolated schools. The Coca-Cola Foundation is the philanthropic arm of the Coca-Cola Company. It joins with organizations around the world to offer grants to support education such as the Valued Youth Program in North America.

Parent Teacher Associations are organized on the national, state and local levels. They award funds to schools and teachers in a host of different ways. The National PTA gives grants to doctorial students for research and writing on topics that cover issues relating to children and education, including matters such as student achievement and assessment, student and parental attitudes and at-risk students. State PTA groups also provide money through grant programs. For example, the California PTA offers grants to help its committees and PTA units, councils and districts to develop and implement parent education and cultural arts programs as well as leadership development. Local school PTA and PTSA organizations may award grants. A popular local grant program provides teachers with funds to reimburse them for the costs of school supplies to be used by students in the classroom.

Professional associations that represent education professionals such as teachers, librarians and administrators may have grant award programs. For example, in 2006, National Education Association members contributed 350,000 books and raised $125,000 for school libraries. Teacher Incentive Grants are offered by the New York State Association of Foreign Language Teachers to its members. Cluster Grants for professional development programs are awarded by the Association of Washington School Principals.

## 2. Getters

As discussed, many "givers" of grants provide funding for a variety of educational purposes. Thus, many "getters" of grants are educational institutions and professionals who receive those grant awards. State Departments of Education receive federal funding to administer various programs. School districts and school boards may receive grants to assist in providing various services. Individual schools may also be awarded grants.

Although many grant givers do not give grant funds to individuals, there are exceptions. Students may win grants to pursue a research project or to fund their college educations. Librarians may receive grants to support their work such as the buying of additional books for their school libraries. Some grants are offered exclusively to teachers for such matters as the creation and administration of classroom projects and to pay for professional development pursuits.

## 3. Teachers, Your Fellow Travelers on Your Granted! Journey

You have learned about the availability of nontraditional funding to support education. You've read about this funding as it applies to grants. You know about grant givers and grant getters and that teachers may be the recipients of grant funds. Now it's time to follow in their footsteps and begin your own journey to write and win grants to support learning in your classroom.

The English author Izaak Walton said, "Good company in a journey makes the way seem shorter." When beginning your grant journey, seek the "good company" of colleagues who have been through the grant process themselves. You probably have teachers or administrators at your school who won classroom grants or who know others who have. Contact them and ask for their suggestions and advice.

You may feel overwhelmed and confused at this point. These "fellow travelers" probably shared your feelings at the beginning of their grant journey. They may have wondered if they could successfully complete the process set forth before them. But, they didn't stop their journey before their destination was in sight. They ventured on and were rewarded for their efforts.

Talk to your teaching colleagues and your school administrators about their experiences with grant writing and winning. They may tell you stories such as the ones that follow.

Cyd Mathis, a former art teacher who now heads a public school English Language Learner (ELL) program, is a "fellow traveler" who tells of her experiences with grants that funded the creation of a "thinking garden" and mosaic murals at her school.

> "The goal of the project was to build a feeling of community among the students and staff and to beautify the school. Every student and staff member was involved in making a piece of the mosaic. At the school dedication there was a strong feeling of pride in our school because we had been involved in a shared experience and the murals and garden were beautiful visual reminders of it."

These projects were created during the first year of Mathis' school. Her principal had a vision that the extensive work involved would bring everyone in the school together––students, parents, faculty– and help form a true community. Without those grants, the school wouldn't have had its beautiful murals and garden, and this feeling of "community" would not have been introduced.

"The project couldn't even be started without the funding that the grant provided. Since our faculty was new and needed some bonding time, having this project was a great thing for them because it pulled us all together. They all seemed very excited about it. The students were eager to be a part of the project because they were able to have a hands-on experience with clay that culminated into a huge, beautiful mural that everyone can enjoy. The idea of having a grant, starting a project, watching the project evolve and then enjoying the beauty of the project has been very rewarding."

Another teacher who sought funding through a teacher grant for a new school is Language Arts teacher Deanna Raab. She discovered her school didn't have the resources to purchase class sets of books necessary to help her students address state reading and writing standards.

A grant can provide funding for a project that not only supports the students who are a part of the initial project funded by the grant, but the materials it purchases can be used by future students as well. Raab's school administration saw the long lasting benefits of the grant she secured. She describes her administration as being "very happy" with the grant award "because it will help the Language Arts department for added resources next year."

Dr. Mai-Lon Wong is a school principal who sees every day the beneficial results of grants obtained by teachers in her school. She says, "Grants are a great way to stimulate the development of innovative projects. Grants help teachers think about their curriculum in creative ways. The writing process helps them to crystallize what they really want to see happen with the project. Grants give teachers courage to try new things." Her teachers have received grant funds for innovative projects from a variety of grant entities, including foundations, nonprofit and for profit corporations and fraternal associations. She jokes that the best advice she can give teachers who are thinking about writing a grant is to "use a catchy title!"

Many principals and administrators show the same support of their teachers' grant writing efforts as Wong displays. She comments, "A principal encouraging a staff member is usually enough to get them to seek a grant, if it is an idea that the teacher supports." Thus, go to your administrator and share your ideas about creation of an innovative project for your classroom. His or her encouragement will be a great foundation for your own grant writing efforts.

Sixth-grade teacher Colleen Collins-Moreno was awarded her first grant during her first year as a teacher. It involved the purchase of several sets of classic novels needed to create a reading club for middle school students at her school. Since it was her first year of teaching, she didn't have supplemental books available for students.

Collins-Moreno says, "Receiving the grant was my first step in building my classroom library and establishing a school-wide reading club for upper grade students." Grant funding can provide teachers with a wide range of materials they need to support learning in their classroom. These needs may be especially acute for first-year teachers, such as Collins-Moreno. She states, "Grants are particularly helpful to first-year teachers. I encourage anyone entering the profession to apply. It costs nothing and can give teachers an opportunity to build much-needed resources in their classrooms!" In fact, the grant award not only provided her with such resources, it was also the basis of her being a finalist for the honor of Rookie Teacher of the Year for her school district. Many new teachers like Collins-Moreno need assistance when beginning their grant journey. *Granted!* offers that assistance to new and experienced teachers alike.

Sometimes high school students are especially difficult to engage in the classroom. Janay Perone, a high school history teacher, was having such difficulties inasmuch as the class textbook didn't present various subjects in a way that held the attention of her students. She envisioned a research project to support her efforts but didn't have classroom materials to offer her students to help them with their research. Perone says one of the most memorable highlights of this experience is the students' reactions to the books they've been using on their projects. "It's a wonderful feeling to see students interested in reading and learning more about a topic." Without the grant, those books would not have been purchased and the students' newfound interest in the subject Perone was teaching would not have existed.

Gina DeCarlo Brown is a Reading Specialist at an elementary school. She has submitted grant applications that resulted in her being awarded funds to purchase books and manipulatives unavailable to her students through regular school channels. These items were used in projects that focused on areas of learning mandated by state academic standards with which her students were struggling. Not only did Brown's students appreciate the new materials available to them because of the grant, but her principal was also "very excited that our school would be receiving money for our students."

Brown was assisted by others in the grant process. Now she feels comfortable enough with the process to write her own grant. Brown advises, "I think it is a matter of someone taking you through the steps and showing you how to do it. If you can have someone take you through the motions once or twice, it will be much easier after that. I am able to write a grant now!"

You may now feel the way these teachers did at the beginning of their grant journeys. You have an idea for a project you would love to have funded but you need some help to begin your own journey to write and win a grant to fund that project. Like the teachers just mentioned, you, too, have "company" on the way. You have the guidance of *Granted! A Teacher's Guide to Writing & Winning Grants* to help you. Read each chapter and follow the suggested process, and you will be closer to your destination–writing and winning your own classroom grant!

# CHAPTER TWO:
# Your *Granted!* Notebook

Granted!

# Getting Organized:
## Ardor and Diligence
## in a Three Ring Binder

Abigail Adams once said, "Learning is not attained by chance, it must be sought for with ardor and attended to with diligence." Her words may have been spoken many years ago, yet they are still relevant today. You are about to begin a journey toward an enhanced learning experience for your students "not attained by chance" but "sought for with ardor and attended to with diligence." The work of this journey will involve writing and winning a grant to fund a project that will promote educational standards in your classroom. Thus, you will be an example of what Abigail Adams said. You know the learning in your classroom won't be left to "chance." Your work in support of their learning will be marked with the ardor and diligence to which Adams alluded.

To help you with the work involved in writing and winning grants, *Granted!* provides information and suggestions to assist you. It will take you step-by-step through a process in which you will be given data about various aspects of the grant process. Then you will be encouraged to research and record data you will use when writing your own grant application. This effort is made easier through the use of worksheets presented throughout the book.

*Granted!* worksheets are for you to use to organize and record your thoughts and data. In this way, they clarify and simplify the grant process. The book includes blank worksheets in the appendix. In addition, sample completed worksheets are included so you can have easy-to-understand examples of how a teacher might use these forms to gather information needed for the grant application process. When you have finished reading *Granted!* and working through the worksheets, you will have the background information necessary to begin your own grant writing and winning process.

# ■ Your *Granted!* Notebook

In order to keep your work organized, place your worksheets into a notebook. This *Granted!* notebook may be divided into sections named after the subject matter covered in the book–the grant process in general and the main elements required in most grant applications in particular. For example, you'll want to put into one section of your notebook all your "Grant Data" such as a worksheet/log of all the grants for which you are applying. Another section of your notebook will contain "Budget" information such as a worksheet containing an itemized listing of the description and cost of all items you are seeking to purchase through a grant.

Thus, your notebook will contain a set of the worksheets found in the book that you have reviewed, completed and arranged by subject. The following list and descriptions of *Granted!* worksheets arranged by subject matter should aid you in creation of your notebook.

## 1. Grant Data

WORKSHEET: **Grant Givers: Ideas and Comments**
Found in Chapter Four

WORKSHEET: **Checklist of Grant Materials**
Found in Chapter Four

WORKSHEET: **Grant Submission Log**
Found in Chapter Four

"Grant Data," the first tab in your notebook, will indicate where to keep various information about the grants you are seeking. It will contain three worksheets. The first worksheet, "Grant Givers: Ideas and Comments," will be a record of your ideas and comments about the entities that give the kind of grants that fund projects like the one you would like to implement in your classroom. The second worksheet, "Checklist of Grant Materials," will be handy to note that you've prepared all that is necessary for your grant submission. "Grant Submission Log," the third worksheet, will allow you to maintain a clear record of all the grants you are seeking.

## 2. Educational Standards

WORKSHEET: **Educational Standards That Need Grant Support**
Found in Chapter Three

WORKSHEET: **Statement of Need**
Found in Chapter Three

WORKSHEET: **SMART Goals**
Found in Chapter Three

Various groups from the U.S. Department of Education to your local school district have formulated educational standards that must be supported in the classroom. The project you wish to fund through a grant will most likely be designed in relation to one or more of these standards. The second tab section of your notebook, "Educational Standards," will contain worksheets that deal with this topic. You will list specific standards that need to be promoted in your classroom in the first worksheet with specific data regarding your needs detailed on the second worksheet. The third worksheet discusses the goals of your project with emphasis on meeting educational standards.

## 3. Project Description

WORKSHEET: **What's Needed in the Classroom**
Found in Chapter Three

WORKSHEET: **Grant Proposal Data**
Found in Chapter Three

WORKSHEET: **School and Student Data**
Found in Chapter Three

Tab three, "Project Description," involves three worksheets that detail various aspects of your project. The first worksheet will describe the items needed to improve learning in your classroom, while the second worksheet relates how those items will help your students meet certain educational standards. In addition, the third worksheet allows you to record various school and student population information most grant applications seek.

## 4. Budget

WORKSHEET: **Proposed Grant Funding: Items/Services**
Found in Chapter Three

WORKSHEET: **Proposed Simple Budget for Grant Project**
Found in Chapter Three
WORKSHEET: **Budget Form**
Found in Chapter Three

WORKSHEET: **Grant Budget**
Found in Chapter Five

WORKSHEET: **Notes on Differences Between Proposed Budget & Actual Purchases**
Found in Chapter Five

WORKSHEET: **Final Budget**
Found in Chapter Five

WORKSHEET: **Distribution of Grant Funds**
Found in Chapter Five

The fourth tab, "Budget," provides a place to put the seven worksheets found in *Granted!* that deal with that

subject. Most grant entities require accurate budgetary data be included in materials submitted to them by

those applying for a grant award. These worksheets help you to do just that. They present various budget

formats, as well as forms for proposed vs. actual grant budgets.

## 5. Evaluation Methodology

WORKSHEET: **Student Survey**
Found in Chapter Three

WORKSHEET: **Observation Log**
Found in Chapter Three

WORKSHEET: **Test Comparison**
Found in Chapter Three

WORKSHEET: **Report/Presentation Rubric**
Found in Chapter Three

WORKSHEET: **Key Findings and Recommendations**
Found in Chapter Three

WORKSHEET: **Grant Evaluation Methodology**
Found in Chapter Five

Granted!

Grant applications may require detailed evaluation procedures regarding measurement of the success or failure of the grant-funded project. Tab five, "Evaluation Methodology," will contain worksheets that provide assistance with the creation and recording of such evaluations.

## 6. Timeline

WORKSHEET: **Narrative Timeline: Sequence of Activities and Associated Timeframes**
Found in Chapter Three

WORKSHEET: **Table Format Project Timeline**
Found in Chapter Three

WORKSHEET: **Teacher Grant Timeline**

WORKSHEET: **Chart Format Project Timeline**
Found in Chapter Three

Grant-funded projects must be created and completed within a certain time period. These timelines can be charted in various ways. The worksheets found in the sixth tab section of your *Granted!* notebook, "Timeline," assist you with this work.

## 7. Publicity and Outreach

WORKSHEET: **Letter of Appreciation**
Found in Chapter Five

WORKSHEET: **Sample Press Release**
Found in Chapter Five

WORKSHEET: **End-of-Project Invitation**
Found in Chapter Five

You may want to publicize your grant and the work of your grant giver, as well as reach out to thank your grant "giver" and those who helped you win your grant award. The three worksheets you place in "Publicity and Outreach," the seventh tab in your notebook, will help you do that.

## 8. Final Reports

WORKSHEET: **Final Report Inquiries**
Found in Chapter Five

WORKSHEET: **Final Report**
Found in Chapter Five

Grant entities often require a "Final Report" be submitted that states details concerning the funded project, such as the final budget, outcomes of evaluation, etc. The first worksheet of tab eight, "Final Reports," lists many of these inquiries while the second worksheet is an example of an actual "Final Report" form.

Before you finish reading *Granted!,* get a notebook and insert subject matter tabs to organize the worksheets you will prepare. Sample completed forms are found in the chapters mentioned in the previous list. However, blank reproducible worksheets are available in the Worksheet Appendix at the end of the book. Copy these worksheets and put them in their appropriate notebook sections. Add your own comments, research, etc., to your notebook. Your *Granted!* notebook will then be a handy tool that organizes your grant data in a way that will be easy to find and work with.

Worksheets are integral components of *Granted!* and will be essential to your *Granted!* notebook. Your day is so filled that having your grant materials in one place will be a great help as you continue your grant journey.

# CHAPTER THREE:
## Your Classroom Project

36

# Starting Your Grant Journey:
## Focus on the Educational Standard that Needs More Classroom Support

Confucius said, "A journey of a thousand miles begins with a single step." With regard to your journey into grant writing and winning, you are about to take that first, single step. Good luck, it should be a rewarding and enlightening trip!

But, what is the first step you should take on this journey to write and win a grant to help your students? Some grant writers may start with finding a grant entity that gives awards to teachers in their geographic areas. Others may start with putting into writing the pet project they have been waiting for years to implement. However, it may be best to look at the "bigger picture" of what's happening with education in general and in your classroom in particular.

There are more and more demands on education to meet prescribed standards. Students are tested and tested through standardized examinations to determine their ability to do well in a variety of subjects. These tests are, in turn, scored pursuant to state and national standards. Schools are then judged by the scores of their students. Teachers are evaluated to see if they are "highly performing" according to standards. The curriculum offered at schools must follow standards established by state and local educational entities.

When you begin your grant journey, think of those standards. You see firsthand the problems your students have in meeting or excelling in the standards imposed on their learning. You no doubt have ideas for projects that would enhance that learning, and you can seek grant funds to implement such projects.

Many grant applications require the teacher seeking the grant to detail the need for his or her proposal. When you think of why your project is needed, think in terms of the academic standards to which those needs relate.

## ■ Educational Standards as the Basis for Your Project's Need

Plato's words, "The beginning is the most important part of the work," still hold true. With that statement in mind, it's important for the success of your grant application to begin your quest correctly. You may have many ideas about what you would like to purchase for your classroom. Maybe you need more reference books, several microscopes or a laptop computer. You know such items would help your students learn in a variety of ways. Students' reports would be better if you had enough dictionaries and thesauruses to allow them easy access to such reference materials. The discussion of cells in your science curriculum would have more meaning if students could actually see cells through the use of a microscope. Your students are learning to speak and write in English, but they need easy access to a classroom computer so they can learn to research on the web to assist in that reading and writing.

All of those goals are worthy, but they should be rooted in educational standards established by your school, district or state education agency. These standards show the real "need" for your project's funding and implementation. For example, you may be a fourth-grade teacher in Arizona. Your students are having grammar, spelling and word usage problems in their writing assignments and tests. You know more dictionaries and thesauruses would help students with their writing assignments. The Arizona Department of Education established writing standards for fourth-grade classes across the state. These standards include what should be required of students regarding the writing process. Some of these requirements set forth the need for students to edit their work through the identification of spelling, grammar and usage errors in their drafts, and the use of resources such as dictionaries and word lists to correct conventions. You want to create a writing project involving the use of dictionaries and thesauruses you would purchase for the classroom. You believe such a project will directly support the state educational standards your curriculum must follow. The purchase of dictionaries and thesauruses is the means to meet the goal of enhanced student performance. But, the actual "need" for your project is based upon support of state writing standards.

Perhaps you are a high school general science teacher in New Jersey who is about to begin a new chapter in your textbook about cells. Your class has no microscopes since the school only supplies them to science classes traditionally considered "laboratory" in nature. You know the purchase of microscopes would aid your students in their understanding of this subject. Your state's Core Curriculum Content Standards for Science include requirements for students regarding the scientific process. All students are to "develop problem-solving, decision-making and inquiry skills, reflected by … conducting systematic observations…" In order to accomplish these standards, students are to be involved in inquiry and problem solving, including the "select[ion] and use [of] the appropriate instrumentation to design and construct investigations [and] show that experimental results can lead to new questions and further investigations." Thus, your idea to purchase classroom microscopes can be based, not only on your observations, but on state mandated core curriculum content standards. The "need" for your proposal is connected to the promotion of these standards.

The final example of a perceived need by a teacher concerns the purchase of a laptop for use in the classroom. Perhaps you are that teacher and your work involves efforts with English Language Learners in a middle school in Minnesota. State reading standards for these ELL students include their being able to understand written English in order to participate in a formal, academic context. These students are to be able to "understand many grade-level texts in a variety of contexts." In the current environment, such "contexts" must include reading materials available for academic research on the Internet. But, you don't have a classroom computer. You know your students have to become familiar with computerized research. Your proposal involves the purchase of a laptop computer and its use by students to research various writing assignments. The need for such a proposal, however, regards support of educational standards.

Consider these examples when you begin to formulate your grant proposal. When you consider the needs of your classroom, think in terms of what educational standards are difficult for your students to meet. State departments of education establish curriculum standards by grade and subject matter. However, other entities may also have standards that relate to learning. For example, the National Council of Teachers of Mathematics have "Curriculum Focal Points" for important topics in mathematics for each grade level, and the New York City Department of Education has promulgated core curriculum and learning standards for its students.

Many grant entities require their grant applicants prove an educational standard mandated by a department of education, school district or education association will be supported through the project they are funding. But, some grant givers never ask for information about educational standards in their applications. These grants are not based on achieving any specific academic standard. They simply require the subject of the grant meet some objective important to the group awarding the grant. For example, the American Farm Bureau's White-Reinhardt Fund for Education offers grants for K-12 classroom projects that increase agricultural literacy. Such grants may have their own "standards" to meet within their guidelines. However, their applications do not refer to academic standards promulgated by educational entities such as state departments of education. Thus, the first step in a journey to write and win such a grant will be to focus on the grant entity's own standard it seeks to support, such as "agricultural literacy."

There are many standards imposed on your students from many different sources. What standard do you find most difficult for your students to meet? Or, perhaps your students are meeting standards but you envision their exceeding those standards if only you could introduce an innovative project to assist them. What would help them to meet or exceed this standard? Do you need additional supplies, books or equipment? Would your students be helped through the work of a visiting professional such as an artist, author or motivational speaker? Focus on educational standards and decide which one needs additional support, and you will be taking the first step on your journey to write and win a grant for your classroom. You will be able to clearly present the academic "need" for your proposed project.

Perhaps you need to research the details of various educational standards before you select the one or ones that relate to your classroom needs. Your school may have a copy of such standards or you may be able to get a copy directly from the entity that established them, such as your school district or state department of education. In addition, you may be able to find your standards online. You may search for education-related websites that link to standards in all states or simply visit the website of the standards group and find a copy of the standards there.

If you are unsure of what standards are mandated in your classroom, you may want to speak to fellow teachers, school administrators or a representative of an educational association. A good place to start is your

Granted!

state department of education website. You should be able to locate the standards of the department there.

When you have found a copy of your standards, you will then be able to determine what educational category involves the greatest need within your classroom. Do your students need the most help with language arts or mathematics or social studies or another subject covered by the standards? Within that category, find specific curriculum content requirements that are especially difficult for your students to meet. Those standards will be the framework upon which your proposal will be based.

For example, the Missouri Department of Education has established educational standards for social studies. Regarding eighth-grade students, the standards state they should possess general knowledge of pre-Columbian cultures, including those of ancient Egypt and Greece. But, your students show no interest in these subjects and the textbook entries are very limited. You have an idea for a hands-on project that would stimulate their learning. However, you teach in a small K-8 school and its media center has very few books on those subjects to supplement what is in your textbook. If you had more books about ancient Egypt and Greece, you could use them as the basis for your project and help make what seems to the students to be a dry subject come to life. Your journey to a grant award to fund a project to buy these books begins with researching the educational standards such a project would support. Focusing on the educational standard will help you begin your efforts to write and win a grant that would fund the purchase of books on ancient Egypt and Greece. So, your first step in your grant journey is to determine what educational standard are most in need of support within your classroom.

Now you, too, can take that first step! A worksheet may help you with your effort, as well as provide a record you can keep with your grant materials for future reference. Review the following sample worksheet regarding educational standards. It lists information about an educational standard in issue in a situation by which a teacher wants to support her sixth-grade students' creative writing efforts. The Worksheet Appendix at the end of *Granted!* includes a blank copy of this worksheet, "Educational Standards That Need Grant Support." Consider what standard needs support in your classroom. Research it, prepare your own worksheet, and place it in your *Granted!* notebook for future reference.

| SAMPLE WORKSHEET: *Educational Standards That Need Grant Support* |
| --- |

**Entity Establishing the Standard:** Arizona State Department of Education

**Web Address:** www.ade.state.az.us

**What standard is difficult to meet within the classroom?**
Writing Standard: Sixth Grade
Strand Three: Writing Applications
Concept 1: Expressive: Expressive writing includes personal narratives, stories, poetry, songs and dramatic pieces. Writing may be based on real or imagined events.
    PO 1. Write a narrative that includes:
        a. an engaging plot based on imagined or real ideas, observations or memories of an event or experience
        b. effectively developed characters
        c. a clearly described setting
        d. dialogue, as appropriate
        e. figurative language or descriptive words and phrases to enhance style and tone
    PO 2. Write in a variety of expressive forms that, according to type of writing, employ:
        a. figurative language
        b. rhythm
        c. dialogue
        d. characterization
        e. plot
        f. appropriate format
Concept 5: Literary Response: Literary response is the writer's reaction to a literary selection. The response includes the writer's interpretation, analysis, opinion and/or feelings about the piece of literature and selected elements within it.
    PO 1. Write a response to literature that:
        a. presents several clear ideas
        b. supports inferences and conclusions with examples from the text

**Where may the standard be found?**
http://www.ade.state.az.us/standards/language-arts/writing/grade6.doc

**Summary of Standard:** Sixth-graders should be applying learned skills to write pieces with expressive content as well as creating written responses to literary selections.

**Why is that standard not being met?**
My students are very creative, but their creativity isn't supported by the routine expressive writing assignments that are currently in the curriculum. In addition, they don't have the opportunity to respond to each other's writing in an organized, literary manner. A more dynamic way of teaching and highlighting student writing is needed.

**Comments/Notes:** Project would be great addition to Creative Writing sessions next semester.

Granted!

## STATEMENT OF NEED

You know what educational standard your students are having difficulty meeting or exceeding. Such evidence as poor grades and lack of classroom participation in matters relating to the subject of that standard indicate this difficulty. You have thought of ways to address those problems. Before you go further on your grant journey, focus on the "statement of need" for the project you wish to have funded.

Many grant givers require your application to include a statement of need. This needs statement may be brief or it may be required to be quite detailed depending on the grant entity's guidelines. Whatever the length, your statement should relate to problems your proposal will address. For example, you may be a high school science teacher whose students come from families with very low incomes. This situation may have an impact on what grant you will apply for since some require the students who will be involved in the teacher's project to be from low income families. However, their "needs" are not the type of "need" referred to in this section of a grant application.

Your students' "needs" may be great, but when you are writing a Statement of Need you should focus on the "problem" these students have in the classroom that your proposal will address. For example, you notice most of your students have difficulty understanding assignments relating to a state science standard concerning describing the characteristics, location and motions of the various kinds of objects in the solar system. You believe a project that would end in a solar system mini-science fair would be a great addition to your curriculum. To support that project, you wish to seek a grant to pay for books on the solar system, star charts and a field trip to your city's planetarium. Without outside funds, this project would be impossible and your "problem" would not be addressed.

A worksheet is included in the Worksheet Appendix that will help you focus on preparation of your Statement of Need. Prepare your own "Statement of Need" and put it in your *Granted!* notebook. The following sample of this worksheet should help. It shows what the teacher in the situation described above might write for her statement.

**State the academic standard your students are having difficulty meeting/exceeding and describe the evidence of that difficulty.**

Most of the 205 students in my high school general science classes are having difficulty with the

curriculum supporting the state science standard for high school students regarding their being

able to understand and describe the characteristics, location and motions of the various kinds of

objects in the solar system. Eighty-two percent of these students made D's or F's on homework

and tests relating to this subject when it was introduced at the beginning of the school year.

Participation in classroom discussions was very low. Students had never used a star chart nor had

they ever visited a planetarium. Thus, it was difficult for them to conceptualize the concepts of the

standard, especially since textbook materials on the subject are quite limited.

# WHAT'S NEEDED TO MEET EDUCATIONAL STANDARDS IN YOUR CLASSROOM

You have written a Statement of Need that sets forth the details of the problem your project will address. This "need" was framed in the difficulty your students are having in meeting or exceeding certain educational standards. You have thought of a project to address these problems. What items must be purchased in order to implement the project? What services need to be contracted?

Some teachers may have problems meeting any standards because their students don't have the school supplies necessary to do their classroom assignments and/or homework. They may simply need pencils, markers, paper, rulers, binders, erasers and the like to help their students. Other teachers may require the purchase of specific items or services to support one especially problematic standard. For example, a geography standard for kindergarten students may require them to know the difference between maps and globes. But, the classroom doesn't have a set of display maps and a globe for the students to study. That kindergarten teacher needs a set of maps and a globe to support that standard in his classroom.

Many classroom projects support educational standards in more indirect ways. For example, reading standards may require students to read and analyze a variety of fiction genres. The school library may have many titles available for reading, but the teacher believes the standard would be better supported if his students read novels together as a class. Thus, he would like class sets representing different fiction genres for use in his classroom. He envisions a project in which his students will read and analyze the books in teams and then report back to the class regarding what they have learned from their efforts. The class sets aren't absolutely required to meet the standard like the purchase of school supplies and maps and a globe in the above examples. However, the sets would greatly enhance his students' ability to not just meet standards, but to excel in the learning they are designed to promote.

You may have wondered many times what you could do to help your students in subjects that are difficult for them to learn. You may also have wondered how you could enhance or highlight their skills and talents in new and innovative ways. But, as Chapter One mentioned, you might have become frustrated with "so many ideas, so little money!" However, money does exist to help you implement those great ideas that will enhance the educational standards supported in your classroom. Grants are available to help you help your students. If you were awarded such a grant, what would you purchase with the funds? What is needed to meet or exceed problematic standards in your classroom?

Think about what supplies, equipment and services could be part of a project to help your students learn. Make a list of your ideas. Categorize the items and estimate their costs and where you would make the purchase or contract for the service. The Worksheet Appendix contains a worksheet, "What's Needed in the Classroom," that will help you with this work.

The following sample worksheet will assist you in determining how to complete the worksheet you will be including in your *Granted!* notebook. It shows what a high school Hospitality Management teacher might prepare to help organize her ideas for what's needed to create and implement a project involving a field trip to a large and a small local hotel. At this point, she received permission from her principal to pursue a grant, and she contacted the hotels about the visit and donating lunches. But, she is simply estimating the cost to charter a bus and buy poster supplies. She believes her students would be helped in the classroom by seeing firsthand the work of real hotel staffs and management. She plans on having them divide into teams that will focus on different aspects of this work. After the trip, these student teams will write a report and create a display regarding what they learned. Class presentations by the teams will follow. This project promotes standards of her state department of education that require her students to be able to explain basic hotel departments and functions.

## SAMPLE WORKSHEET: *What's Needed in the Classroom*

**Educational Standard to be Supported:** Hospitality Standard: Explain Basic Hotel Departments and Functions

| Items Needed | Description/Quantity | Price Estimate | Where to Purchase |
|---|---|---|---|
| Field Trip to Two Local Hotels | Rental of one bus for five hours | $500 | Lots of Buses Transportation Co |
| Supplies | 10 display poster boards | $50 | Local Office Supply Store |
| Equipment | NA | | |
| Computer/Hardware/Software | NA | | |
| Media (CD, DVD, etc.) | NA | | |
| Other | 33 lunches | $0 | Donated by Hotel |
| Professional Services | NA | | |
| | | | |

| Comments/Notes: |
|---|
| Grant needed for transportation; Principal & School District trip approval already secured |

# Your Project: *Needed Support to Meet Educational Standards in Your Classroom*

You have taken that first step toward writing and winning your classroom grant. You identified the educational standard your students are having difficulty meeting and wrote a Statement of Need. You listed items and services that would help your students regarding that standard. Now you are ready to design a project that will address your classroom needs.

## ■ Doing Your Homework: *Talk with Administration, Fellow Teachers, Students*

The baseball player Roger Maris said, "You win not by chance, but by preparation," and you are on track with your grant preparations. Continue your efforts by talking to others about your ideas and get their ideas as well.

Your project will be designed to help your students. Why not ask them what they think would help them meet problematic standards? You may also want their feedback on your project ideas. You may want to formally survey your students about these matters or wait until your project has been awarded a grant. You can then survey your students about the subject of the project. Those surveys may then become part of a grant evaluation process, which will be discussed later in the chapter.

As mentioned in Chapter One, input from fellow teachers can be very helpful. Perhaps one has received a grant in the past and will be able to give valuable insight. Other teachers may have had the same problems in their classrooms as you have had. They may have thought about solutions to these problems that will help you determine how you want to proceed with your project.

The grant you apply for will probably require your principal or another administrator to sign off on its application. Before you begin the first draft of your proposal is a good time to speak with him or her about your desire to apply for a grant as well as the subject of the project it would fund. Your principal may have been part of past grant efforts and know of grant entities involved in funding projects at your school or in your school district in the past. He or she may also provide guidance on how to best approach the subject and how to follow any applicable rules and regulations. For example, your school may have a policy that all grant funds must be deposited in, and distributed from, school accounts even if the grant is awarded in the teacher's name. Many other matters of importance may come up during a meeting with your principal. Try to schedule one as soon as possible. When the meeting takes place, be sure to take notes and include them in your *Granted!* notebook.

## ■ Project Details

You have done your "homework" and are now ready to draft a description of the project you envision will help your students improve their learning. You know what your project will involve and what academic standard establishes the need for it. You have thought about items and services that must be purchased to help your students meet this standard. You are now ready to flesh out the details of your proposal.

### PROJECT DESCRIPTION

Begin with a narrative description. The length of that description will depend on the requirements of the grant application. Some grants expect an extensive description of every aspect of your project. Other grants have a very abbreviated application process and may only require a paragraph long description. Some want a mere summary of the project. Others expect details of the workings of the project and exact information regarding the future use of every item purchased through the grant, even after the completion of the project. At this point, you are merely recording your ideas and not applying for a grant. Thus, prepare your project description with the idea that it is a draft that may be edited pursuant to the guidelines of the grant for which you will be applying.

The "Grant Proposal Data" worksheet in Chapter Two may now be completed and put within your *Granted!* notebook. As you consider the basic facts concerning your project, think of the standard that establishes the need and focus for it. Write a short statement of that standard. Then give a brief description of the project. Review what you've written. Think of a name that will provide the grant entity with some insight into your project and be a "hook" the grant selection committee will remember among the many projects it reviews.

The sample worksheet should assist with this process. It is a description of a proposal to support a social science standard regarding a study of the Middle Ages.

| SAMPLE WORKSHEET: *Grant Proposal Data* |
| --- |
| **1. Standard:** |
| Social Science/Analysis of cultural achievement in the Medieval period |
| **2. Brief Description of Project:** |
| Seventh grade social studies students will form teams to study various aspects of medieval life including castles, knighthood, the plague, the Knights Templar and serfdom.  They will read books on these topics to be purchased through grant money and write related reports.  They will prepare trifold poster boards, also purchased with grant funds, with information regarding their assigned subject. They will be presented to the class, as well as parents, teachers, administrators and grant personnel who will be invited into the classroom. Students will create simple medieval costumes to wear during their presentations. The event will be called "The Guild Fair." |
| **3.  Name of Project and Comments if Applicable:** |
| THE GUILD. Craftsmen and artisans formed labor associations called guilds during the middle ages, the time period students are studying.  They will also be laboring as a team on their medieval life projects. The teacher will discuss guilds as a spring board to THE GUILD project. |
| |

## "SMART" PROJECT GOALS

You established the need for your project in terms of better meeting educational standards. The *Merriam-Webster Dictionary* defines a "need" as a lack of something requisite, desirable or useful. Your project is something "requisite, desirable or useful" to the meeting of standards in your classroom. Thus, you know the "need" for your project. But, what are your project's goals?

The *American Heritage Dictionary* defines a "goal" as the "purpose toward which an endeavor is directed; an objective." What is the objective of your project? What specifically do you want to accomplish, and how will you determine whether or not these accomplishments have been realized? Peter Drucker, educator and business writer, said, "Objectives are not fate; they are direction. They are not commands; they are commitments." In that way, the objectives or goals you set for your project are not the final word on what you want to accomplish. They simply show the direction you want that project to take and that you are committed to the work necessary to accomplish those goals.

You are committed to help your students better meet educational standards through your project. Now you should set forth the goals for that proposal. Some grant applications require the submission of goals for the project proposal in the grant application. There are many ways you can approach the writing of your project goals. You may want to rely on the "SMART" method when stating your project's objectives. This project management technique is based on the writings of Peter Drucker over 50 years ago. This method offers a format for recording information about your project goals. In that regard, review the following SMART format in relation to your proposal:

## SPECIFIC
Is there a specific outcome you believe your project will achieve?

## MEASURABLE
Do you have a way to measure whether or not your project meets this outcome?

## ACHIEVABLE
Are the outcomes you seek really achievable?

## RELEVANT
Is your goal relevant to the needs of your students?

## TIME-BOUND
Is the achievement of your goal part of a process with a beginning and ending date?

To help you organize your thoughts, prepare your "SMART Goals" by using the appropriate worksheet mentioned in Chapter Two (see Worksheet Appendix for blank form) and then including it in your *Granted!* notebook. The following sample worksheet shows how goals might be described by a teacher seeking a grant to fund the purchase of workbooks and math manipulatives to help her students learn their multiplication tables.

**S (Specific Goals)** _____ Each student will complete the multiplication workbook and perform daily exercises using math manipulatives.

_____

_____

_____

_____

**M (Measurable)** _____ 70% of students should score 80% or higher on a test covering multiplication tables after completion of the project.

_____

_____

_____

**A (Achievable)** _____ Grant funding will allow for the purchase of workbooks and manipulatives to be used by students during established daily classroom math sessions.

_____

_____

_____

**R (Realistic)** _____ The introduction of reinforcement of multiplication principles through workbook exercises and manipulative work will make measurable goals realistic.

_____

_____

_____

**T (Time-Bound)** _____ The workbook and manipulatives will be used in daily math sessions over a period of two months with a test over the subject at the end of the two months.

_____

_____

_____

# PROPOSED BUDGET

A vital element of any grant proposal is its budget. Grant entities require a detailed statement of the budget proposed to purchase the items and services necessary to implement the grant project. You have already considered what should be purchased to better support learning standards your students have difficulty meeting. Review the worksheet, "What's Needed in the Classroom," on which you wrote those ideas. This work will now be the basis for your preparation of a proposed budget that will contain data regarding these items/ services and any other purchases needed for your project.

As with other steps in the grant process, the form of this proposed budget must follow the guidelines and requirements of the grant entity. But, it is important at this stage of your grant journey to create a proposed budget before you begin to search for the right grant entity to fund your project. If your proposal indicates you need more than $5,000 to fund your project, you may not want to apply for a $500 grant unless you apply in order to fund only a portion of your project. In that case, you must study the grant guidelines to see if funds are available only for payment of all aspects of a proposal.

Now you are ready to finalize the details of needed items and services by determining the cost and source of each entry. For example, if you want a class set of novels, contact the bookstore you want to purchase them from and record details of your proposed order; e.g., title, author, ISBN, binding, cost per book and total cost, tax and shipping. If you are seeking professional services such as a class visit from an author, be sure to contact that author and determine the cost involved in such a visit and his or her availability, and record the information.

Note: You may need to find items through an approved vendor list created by your school district, and any professional may need to be on a similarly approved guest artist list. If you do not know if such procedures are required, be sure to speak to a school administrator. In addition, your grant entity may or may not have similar requirements. Be sure to familiarize yourself with its requirements before you apply for one of its grants. In addition, determine the prices you list are fair and reasonable. Many vendors offer discounts to teachers. Take advantage of these lowered prices when formulating your budget.

Don't stop with just a list of what you'll need to purchase with grant funds to implement your project. Other items and services might be available through non-grant sources. Will you need parent volunteers to help with your project? Will your school provide supplies and printing? Will your school's PTA match any funds you obtain through a grant? Are you attempting to win grants from more than one entity? Is a local store willing to donate any items on your list? These matters relate to "in kind" support for the project for which you are seeking grant funds. They will not require money from your grant entity, but they still should be a part of your budget. In fact, many grant entities require such support outside of its grant award. Again, check grant guidelines.

Your "What's Needed in the Classroom" worksheet was a record of your thoughts and estimates. Now you need to list the details of the items/services you are actually seeking funding for through your grant application. Go to the Worksheet Appendix and review the budget worksheets. Use the one that best matches your proposal.

Following are sample worksheets to assist you with developing your proposed budget. The teacher in the worksheets wants to create a computerized music composition project. She first prepared a "What's Needed in the Classroom" worksheet based on what she wanted to implement with her project. She asked some friends about the information but didn't check out these estimates and didn't finalize the prices. As she continued to develop her project, contact other teachers and research prices online and through calls to local vendors, she found some of her original estimates were incorrect. She also discovered a computer store selling laptops for a lower price than the original cost she noted. With this new information, she prepared the sample "Proposed Grant Funding: Items/Services" worksheet. It is the finalized version of the estimates and thoughts contained in her "What's Needed in the Classroom" worksheet. Also included in this budget worksheet are the sources of funding for the purchase of each item or service listed. With this finalized listing, the teacher will be ready to prepare a budget for the grant application she will ultimately submit.

Review and compare her "What's Needed in the Classroom" worksheet to the "Proposed Grant Funding" worksheet she later completed. You may also discover your initial considerations may need revision before you enter the related information on your final budget document.

## SAMPLE WORKSHEET: *What's Needed in the Classroom*

**Educational Standard to be Supported:** Music Standard: Composition and Arrangement

| Items Needed | Description/Quantity | Price Estimate | Where to Purchase |
|---|---|---|---|
| Books | Writing Music on the Computer by Connie Composer | 30 copies @ $14.95 each | Connies website |
| Supplies | Music Composition Paper, 500 sheets | $20 | Connie's Website |
| Equipment | NA | | |
| Computer/Hardware | laptop computer/1 | $1,800 | Big Store |
| Computer Software | software to assist with composition/1 | $250 | Big Store |
| Media (CD, DVD, etc.) | blank CDs/100 | $50 | Big Store |
| Other | NA | | |
| Professional Services | Connie Composer/will demonstrate | $1,000 | Connie's Website |

**Comments/Notes:**

grant needed; nothing to support teaching computerized composition

# SAMPLE WORKSHEET: *Proposed Grant Funding: Items/Services*

| Items/Service | Description | Qty | Cost Each | Shipping | Tax | Total | Vendor | Funding Source |
|---|---|---|---|---|---|---|---|---|
| **Books** | | | | | | | | |
| Writing Music on the Computer | paperback, ISBN 0000000000 | 25 | 12.95 | 20.00 | 25.90 | 323.75 | www.conniecomposer.info | GRANT ENTITY |
| by Connie Composer | | | | | | | | |
| | | | | | | | | |
| **Supplies** | | | | | | | | |
| music composer paper | | 500 | | .80 | 1.28 | | www.conniecomposer.info | GRANT ENTITY |
| | | | | | | | | |
| | | | | | | | | |
| **Computer Equipment** | | | | | | | | |
| XYZ Notebook Laptop Computer | | 1 | 1200.00 | | 96.00 | | Big Computer Store | GRANT ENTITY |
| | | | | | | | | |
| | | | | | | | | |
| **Computer Software** | | | | | | | | |
| ConnieMusicMaker software | | 1 | 250.00 | 10.00 | 20.00 | | www.conniecomposer.info | GRANT ENTITY |
| | | | | | | | | |
| | | | | | | | | |
| **Media** | | | | | | | | |
| blank music CDs | | 100 | 20.00 | | | | store | GRANT ENTITY |
| **Other** | | | | | | | | |
| 15 hours of assistance in the classroom | | | | | | | 3 parent volunteers | |
| **Professional Services** | | | | | | | | |
| Connie Composer demonstrate | $100 per hour for 10 hours | | 1000.00 | | | | www.conniecomposer.info | GRANT ENTITY |
| computerized composition and assist for | | | | | | | | |
| two days in the classroom | | | | | | | | |

This teacher now has enough information to prepare a final budget for her grant application. The exact form of that budget will depend on what's required by the grant giving entity.

Budget forms differ greatly. Some, especially for grants for under $1,000, may be fairly simple to prepare. For example, a teacher who is trying to win a grant to buy classroom books and supplies may be able to apply for that grant with a mere statement of the description of the items and their costs. The following sample worksheet contains this type of simple budget. A blank copy of the worksheet is found in the Worksheet Appendix for your use if you are preparing a simple budget document.

| SAMPLE WORKSHEET: *Proposed Simple Budget* | | | |
|---|---|---|---|
| Funding Requested for Purchase of: | QTY | Price | Vendor |
| Books: | | | |
| *Genetics and DNA* by AB See | 35/$19.95 ea | $698.25 | 123 Bookstore |
| ISBN 000000000, hardcover | | | address |
| | | | |
| Supplies: | | | |
| Poster Boards | 35/$1 ea | $35.00 | 456 Mart |
| | | | address |
| | | | |
| | | | |
| | | | |
| | | | |
| | | | |
| | | | |
| | | | |
| | | | |
| | | | |
| | | | |
| | | | |
| | | | |
| | Subtotal | $733.25 | |
| | Tax | 46.20 | |
| | **Total Funds Requested** | $804.20 | |

Other grant entities may require more complex budget documents and even provide sample forms on their websites. These forms may require information not only on the way grant funds are to be spent, but also on any matching and "in kind" support for your project. These grant givers may require the funds they award to be matched by other groups. Such information would then have to be made a part of the project budget. For example, parents could provide matching funds for your project through a school-wide fundraiser. The amount they raised would be noted in the budget. Grant entities may also require budget entries for any "in kind" support such as donated supplies, office space and volunteer services. As always, check your grant entity's guidelines to see what it defines as "matching funds" and "in kind" support and whether those matters must be made a part of the project budget.

The Worksheet Appendix provides additional blank budget worksheets so you can choose which is best to include in your *Granted!* notebook. If these forms aren't appropriate, add your own. The following sample worksheet, "Budget Form," may be helpful to show what type of budget document may be required of you if your grant entity has an online form you must use. In the sample, the teacher is applying for a grant to fund a school-wide dramatic arts project that will involve teacher training, artist mentors, field trips and paid admissions to theater performances. Note: The "Supported By" section shows the project is supported by the grant entity, a parent sponsored fundraiser and school and local business donations.

| SAMPLE WORK SHEET: *Budget Form* | | |
|---|---|---|
| **Budget Category/Explanation** | **Amount** | **Supported By** |
| **Cash Expenses:** | | |
| **Fees to Artists/Organizations** | | |
| Teacher Training - 5 hrs @ $50/hr | $250 | **Grant Entity** |
| Artist Mentors - 100 hrs @ $50/hr | $5,000 | **Grant Entity** |
| Field Trips - 5 @ $625 | $3,125 | Parent Sponsored Fundraiser |
| Performances - 2 @ $2,000 | $4,000 | **Grant Entity** |
| **Fees to Coordinators / Consultants** | | |
| Consultant - 25 hrs @ $50/hr | $1,250 | **Grant Entity** |
| **Materials / Administrative Expenses** | | |
| Supplies | $150 | **Grant Entity** |
| **Transportation & Other Expenses** | | |
| Student transportation | $1,850 | Parent Sponsored Fundraiser |
| Artist / Consultant transportation | $200 | **Grant Entity** |
| **TOTAL CASH EXPENSES** | **$15,825** | |
| | | |
| **Cash Income:** | | |
| Grant Entity Name | $10,850 | **Grant Entity** |
| Parents | $4,975 | Parents |
| **TOTAL CASH INCOME** | **$15,825** | |
| | | |
| **In-Kind Support:** | | |
| Office expenses/printing | $500 | School |
| Supplies | $500 | Local Art Shop |
| **TOTAL IN-KIND SUPPORT** | **$1,000** | |
| | | |
| Budget Summary: | | |
| **Grant Request** | **$10,850** | *Amount requested from Grant Entity* |
| Cash Match | $4,975 | *Cash Income not including grant funds* |
| In-Kind Support | $1,000 | *Total donated services/materials* |
| **TOTAL PROJECT BUDGET** | **$16,825** | *Sum of above* |
| | | |
| | | |
| | | |
| | | |
| | | |

# SCHOOL AND STUDENT DATA

You are well on your way to developing your grant plan. You have considered the academic standard you wish to support, described your project and its goals and prepared a budget. Now focus on your school and your students. Many grant entities require this information. Some limit their grant awards to projects that involve certain types of students or schools. For example, some grants are designed to fund programs only in public schools, and the funds from others are to be used only in support of projects for low income students. You may need your school's tax number, diversity statistics of your students, etc. to provide needed documentation.

Take this opportunity to record such information. The "School and Student Data" worksheet in the Worksheet Appendix will help you create such a record and should be placed in your *Granted!* notebook. The following sample worksheet shows how this might be done.

| SAMPLE WORKSHEET: *School and Student Data* |
| --- |
| **SCHOOL DATA** |
| Name:  Apple High School |
| Address:  78 South 9th Ave., My Town, USA 00000 |
| School District:  Blackboard Unified School District |
| Fax:  000-000-0000 |
| Phone:  000-000-0000 |
| Website:  www.applehighschool.com |
| Principal:  Aca Demic |
| Tax Number:  0 |
| Type of Institution:  (e.g., public, private, charter) |
| Grades Taught:  9 - 12 |
| Number of Students:  2,517 |
| Title I:  902 |
| Diversity Statistics:  15% Hispanic; 10% African American; 5% Native American; 70% Caucasian |
| Other Information: |
| |
| **STUDENT DATA** (regarding those to be involved in grant-funded project) |
| Grade(s):  10th |
| Age(s):  15-16 years old |
| Number Impacted by Grant Project: 125 |
| Title I:  35 |
| Diversity Statistics:  same as school |
| Other Information: |

# ■ Evaluation Methodology

You have developed your project, but your grant entity will want to know if it met your expectations. Were the goals of the project realized? Did it support the academic standard as you thought it would? If problems arose, what can be learned and how can these problems be corrected in the future? The implication of such questions is that the money award through your grant should have been wisely spent. You should incorporate an evaluation process with your grant proposal in order to show the grant entity you will be able to answer such questions.

The methodology of your evaluation process may be as simple or complex as is required by the grant entity. Be sure you follow any guidelines your grant giver establishes for how to evaluate your grant funded project. Some methods are qualitative, such as determining the level of interest of your students regarding your classroom project. Others may be quantitative, such as calculating the number of students involved in your project. Evaluation methods may include:

- **pre- and post-project interviews**
- **pre- and post-project surveys**
- **pre- and post-project testing**
- **teacher observations**
- **student reports and presentations**
- **key findings and recommendations**

Worksheets on each method are provided in the Worksheet Appendix. Review them as you begin to develop your own evaluation methodology. This chapter contains samples of completed evaluation worksheets in order to help you decide which methodology you will include in your proposal, as well as how you will complete your evaluation once your grant is awarded. Prepare your own evaluation-related worksheets and put them in your *Granted!* notebook to help you during the application process.

## INTERVIEWS/SURVEYS

Interviews of students, parents, administrators and/or fellow teachers may be conducted regarding their thoughts on present curriculum dealing with the standard in question. Relate the details of your project in the interviews and then follow up with a second round of interviews after the project is completed. The survey process is similar except the questions are formalized into a written format. You may want to interview your principal during a meeting about your grant ideas while a survey of students may be the better way to record the responses of that large group.

The Worksheet Appendix includes a blank worksheet regarding a survey. Following is a sample of that "Student Survey" worksheet to help you complete your own. In this situation, a teacher is surveying her students regarding their feelings about the writing component of her Language Arts class. Their responses will help her formulate and evaluate her proposal in support of academic writing standards.

| SAMPLE WORKSHEET: *Student Survey* |
|---|

Teacher: Mr Jones

Date: _____

## What do you think of your writing class?

**Circle the number that is closest to how you feel about the statement. If you don't know or don't have an opinion, circle the X.**

5  Strongly Agree
4  Agree
3  Neutral (neither agree nor disagree)
1  Strongly Disagree
X  Don't know / No Opinion

| | Don't Know/ No Opinion | Strongly Disagree | Disagree | Neutral | Agree | Strongly Agree |
|---|---|---|---|---|---|---|
| 1. Writing is my favorite subject at school. | X | 1 | 2 | 3 | 4 | 5 |
| 2. I make good grades in Writing Class. | X | 1 | 2 | 3 | 4 | 5 |
| 3. I enjoy writing. | X | 1 | 2 | 3 | 4 | 5 |
| 4. It's easy to come up with good ideas to write about. | X | 1 | 2 | 3 | 4 | 5 |
| 5. I use good grammar when writing. | X | 1 | 2 | 3 | 4 | 5 |
| 6. I need extra help with my writing assignments. | X | 1 | 2 | 3 | 4 | 5 |
| 7. I like to have others read what I write. | X | 1 | 2 | 3 | 4 | 5 |
| 8. My writing assignments are challenging. | X | 1 | 2 | 3 | 4 | 5 |
| 9. My writing assignments are fun. | X | 1 | 2 | 3 | 4 | 5 |
| 10. I am proud of my writing. | X | 1 | 2 | 3 | 4 | 5 |

Granted! ⬅️🖎

A comparison of such methods before and after the project is one way to evaluate the proposal. For example, a teacher could survey students about their challenges with, and attitudes about, learning geography. Then the teacher could survey them on these topics after the completion of the geography-related project and compare the two surveys' results. If challenges are better met and attitudes more responsive after the project, this is an indication of a positive outcome for the project.

## TESTING

Testing is a common method of evaluation. If a teacher is seeking a grant to buy math manipulatives for her second-grade class to assist with their learning multiplication, she could compare their math grades before the project to those after the project. In addition, some teachers may want to include standardized test scores as a method of evaluation of their project. If their project involved the writing component of such a test, they would compare scores of students in that area before and after the project designed to improve their writing skills.

The comparison of test scores is a clear, quantitative evaluation method as seen in the "Test Comparison" worksheet in the Worksheet Appendix. Following is a sample of that worksheet for a teacher whose project involves support of reading comprehension standards.

| SAMPLE WORKSHEET: *Test Comparison* | | |
|---|---|---|
| **Grade Log: Reading Comprehension** | | |
| (List names of each student.) | (List comprehension test grades before and after project.) Grade: | |
| Student Name: | Pre-Project Test | Post-Project Test |
| Mary Brown | 75% | 90% |
| Jerrod Green | 60% | 75% |
| Deborah Red | 88% | 88% |
| Juan Blue | 95% | 98% |
| Tamika Turquoise | 80% | 92% |
| Nick Silver | 65% | 72% |
|  |  |  |
|  |  |  |
|  |  |  |
|  |  |  |
|  |  |  |
| Average Grades for Class: | 77% | 87% |

# OBSERVATIONS

A teacher learns a lot from classroom observations. These observations may be reduced to writing and offer an evaluation of the grant project. What is the degree of student involvement before, during and after the project? These observations may produce a quantifiable tool for evaluating the grant project if the teacher assigns numeric values to such "involvement" as seen in the "Observation Log" worksheet in the Worksheet Appendix.

The sample "Observation Log" that follows shows a portion of such a worksheet completed by a drama teacher who wants to quantify her students' participation in the classroom during discussions during each day of her project.

| SAMPLE WORKSHEET: *Observation Log* | | |
|---|---|---|
| **Project:** Mrs. Smith's Shakespeareans | | |
| **Date:** April 15, 2009 | | |
| **Observation:** Student participated in class discussion, offered ideas, listened to others and stayed on task. | | |
| **Score Scale:** 5 Strongly Agree / 4 Agree / 3 Neutral (neither agree nor disagree) / 2 Disagree / 1 Strongly Disagree / X Student Absent | | |
| **Student Name:** | **Score:** | **Comments:** |
| Jane Doe | 5 | Leads discussions, offers new ideas, on task |
| Jill Roe | 2 | Offers nothing but listens to others |
| Bill Moe | X | Absent |
| | | |
| | | |
| | | |
| | | |
| | | |
| | | |

# REPORTS/PRESENTATIONS

After studying the subject matter of your grant project, you may decide to assign your students written reports and oral presentations as components to the proposal. The grades of such assignments could be compared to grades given on similar assignments prior to the project implementation. In addition, the project may rely on students working together in teams in ways they did not before the project. The success of such "teamwork" could also be noted by the teacher as part of this evaluation process.

Chapter Two's worksheet, "Report/Presentation Rubric," which can be found in the Worksheet Appendix, offers a method that may be used as a tool to quantify outcomes of both your students' work and the impact of your project. A sample worksheet follows that presents a rubric used by a teacher for grading student presentations that were part of a poetry reading project.

## SAMPLE WORKSHEET: *Poetry Reading Rubric*

NAME OF STUDENT: Billy Bill

DATE: September 22, 2

| Criteria | 4 | 3 | 2 | 1 | POINTS |
|---|---|---|---|---|---|
| Poetic Devices | Two or more poetic devices are used and fully developed | One poetic device is used and fully developed | One poetic device is used but not fully developed | No poetic devices used | 3 |
| Ideas | Innovative and interesting ideas presented in the poem | Ideas are clear and focused but not presented in an interesting manner | Ideas are understandable but presented randomly | Ideas presented are unclear and unfocused | 4 |
| Presentation | Poem read with expression and appropriate voice | Poem read with expression but in a hurried or inappropriate voice | Difficult to understand student when reading poem | Poem not read before the class | 3 |
| | | | | | |
| | | | | | |
| | | | | | |

**TOTAL POINTS:** 10 of 12 possible          **Grade:** 83.3%

# KEY FINDINGS/RECOMMENDATIONS

Evaluation of a project should include key findings and recommendations. What was discovered through your project? Were students better able to meet academic standards? The primary matter to be evaluated in any project is whether or not it met its goals. Your project sought to support your students' ability to meet certain educational standards. Were these standards supported? The evaluation methodology you include in your project proposal will help to answer this question. Your project may have had a positive impact on your students' learning, or perhaps it had no significant, or even a negative, impact. All outcomes must be recorded.

Finally, recommendations should come from those key findings. If problems arose under the project, how could they be corrected in the future? If the project was successful, how can its success be introduced into future classroom situations? If you purchased books and equipment with your grant money, how will their use be continued? If you paid for the services of a professional, how can the work he or she began continue? Grant entities want to know their funds did not support a single effort but will have a lasting impact on future classes. Check out worksheet "Key Findings and Recommendations" in the Worksheet Appendix as an example of a record of these findings.

The following sample worksheet regards a reading project that had two positive "key findings" which lead the teacher to recommend continuation of the program.

| SAMPLE WORKSHEET: *Key Findings and Recommendations* ||
|---|---|
| **KEY FINDINGS** | **RECOMMENDATIONS** |
| 1.Students' scores on reading comprehension exams | School Reading Specialist's use of books, |
| improved by 20% after completion of exercises and | flash cards, phonics CDs and videos |
| lessons of reading project | should continue |
|  |  |
| 2. 50% of students improved their scores on |  |
| standardized reading tests after completion |  |
| of reading project. |  |
|  |  |

# ◼ TIMELINE

Y ou have worked to prepare each step of your journey toward winning a grant to promote learning in your classroom. To assist you in the process and to show the grant entity what is involved in each step of your project and when each step will be taken, you should prepare a timeline for submission with your grant application.

As with other grant elements, check with your grant entity's guidelines to see if a form is provided for this effort. If not, list the steps needed to complete your project and the dates by which they are to be accomplished. If you are working with others, list who is responsible for completion of each step. Worksheets showing timelines prepared in narrative, table and chart formats are in the Worksheet Appendix. Sample worksheets follow per different formats in order to give you ideas regarding how you might want to prepare your project's timeline.

The first sample timeline reflects an informal, narrative process of reporting details of the steps taken in fulfillment of a project regarding the purchase of library books. These books are to be used by a school's kindergarten and first-grade students, whose reading scores indicate they are having problems meeting reading standards for their grade levels.

| SAMPLE WORKSHEET: |
|---|
| **Narrative Timeline: *Sequence of Activities and Associated Timeframes*** |

| DATE: | ACTIVITY: |
|---|---|
| December 15: | Foundation advises school of grant funding for "Literacy Library" for emergent readers and funding received via check issued to school |
| December 18: | Committee of Principal, Media Specialist, kindergarten and first-grade teachers and two representative parent volunteers formed to select titles for purchase; Principal deposits check into school account |
| December 20: | Committee Meeting: reviews kindergarten and first-grade reading scores, surveyed as to areas of need and selects books for project; Books ordered by Principal for "Literacy Library" and paid for through school credit card |
| December 20: | Media Specialist writes and distributes Press Release regarding grant award to local papers and writes letter of appreciation to Foundation |
| January 20: | In-service for kindergarten and first-grade teachers and parent volunteers who will assist with small reading groups regarding the literacy library and its uses |
| January 22: | Books received by Media Specialist, prepared for checkout and placed in Media Center |
| January 22: | Kindergarten and first-grade teachers review relevant reading scores and form small reading groups of students with low scores; Assistance of parent volunteers begins |
| January 22: | Books distributed to appropriate classrooms and reading groups begin to use them |
| January-April 20: | Reading groups continue and "Literacy Library" books circulate among kindergarten and first-grade classrooms as needed |
| January-April 20: | Use of books and reading group activities tracked by Media Specialist |
| April 20: | Media Specialist reports book use and reading group activities to Principal |
| April 20: | Students tested; Teachers review post-project reading scores and classroom activities of students in small reading groups vs. those not in such reading groups and report findings to Media Specialist and Principal |
| April 25: | Media Specialist prepares Final Report on project; Principal reviews and approves |
| On or before May 10: | Submission of Final Report to Foundation |

Granted!

Instead of this narrative format, you may want to prepare your timeline in a table format. You may prefer putting your timeline in this format or it may be the one provided in your grant entity's online application and must, therefore, be used. The following sample table shows the timeline for a project to purchase computer software for a high school calculus class.

| SAMPLE WORKSHEET: **Table Format Project Timeline** | | | | |
|---|---|---|---|---|
| **Objective:** Develop and Implement a semester long study of the use of software to assist students in their understanding of calculus. | | | | |
| Activity | Do What? | By Whom? | When? | Challenges Expected |
| 1. Grant Award | Receive award at PTA meeting; letter of appreciation written/ mailed; Press Release through Principal's office | Teacher | September 22 | none |
| 2. Pre-Project Testing and Surveying of Students; Introduce Students to Project | Test students on chapters 1-3 of text; survey them on computer experience and ideas to incorporate computerized study into the classroom; explain grant project and its goals | Students; Teacher | September 25 - 30 | Students may have varying computer experience |
| 3. Purchase of software; Begin its use in the classroom | Purchase software at XYZ Computer Store; Reserve school computer lab on Mondays, Tuesdays and Wednesdays throughout semester; begin software demonstrations | Teacher | October 2 - 5 | Already made arrangements for store to accept endorsed grant check |
| 4. Students begin working with software; observation of student involvement | Students in computer lab Mondays – Wednesdays; teacher records Observation Log | Students; Teacher | October - December | Traditional classroom for review and testing |
| 5. Post-project testing and student surveys | Students tested on materials studied pursuant to computer project; students surveyed regarding their involvement | Students; Teacher | December 5 - 10 | Share results with dept. chair |
| 6. Evaluations | Compare pre- and post-project tests and surveys; analyze Observation Log per test and surveys | Teacher | December 11 - 15 | none |
| 7. Final Report | Prepare Final Report and meet with Principal and Dept. Chair regarding Its Content | Teacher | December 16 | Be sure Principal & Chair are available |
| 8. Recommendations | Prepare recommendation for Principal and Dept. Chair re: outcomes of project and possible future use of software; copy and mail Final Report to PTA | Teacher | December 18 | Follow up next semester |

Another way to present your timeline is through the use of a chart such as the one in the following sample worksheet.

**SAMPLE WORKSHEET: *Chart Format Project Timeline***

| Activity: | 12-Feb | 15-Feb | 21-Feb | Feb-Mar | Mar 12-15 | 10-Mar | 25-Mar | 28-Mar | 5-Apr | 12-Apr |
|---|---|---|---|---|---|---|---|---|---|---|
| Grant award & funds deposit | ▓ | | | | | | | | | |
| Books & supplies purchased | | ▓ | | | | | | | | |
| Explain project to students & distribute books | | | ▓ | | | | | | | |
| Reading groups formed; reading & discussion | | | | ▓ | | | | | | |
| Work on group presentations | | | | | ▓ | | | | | |
| Reception invitation: parents, administration, grant director | | | | | | ▓ | | | | |
| Presentations given at reception | | | | | | | ▓ | | | |
| Tests given; test & presentation graded | | | | | | | | ▓ | | |
| Discuss Final Report with administrator | | | | | | | | | ▓ | |
| Final Report completed & mailed | | | | | | | | | | ▓ |

Granted!

No matter which format you use, be sure to follow your timeline throughout your grant process. Tack it on a classroom bulletin board or tape it to the top of your desk. Just be sure to keep it available for you to refer to so you'll be sure to stay on track. Your efforts will help you to write a Final Report, required by many grant givers, as well as your recommendations for the future of your project.

You have focused on the educational standards that show the need for your project and you have developed all the details surrounding it. You are now ready to find the right grant that matches your proposal!

# CHAPTER FOUR:
## Finding the Right Grant for Your Project

74

# The Match Game:
## Matching Your Proposal to Available Grants

T here never is but one opportunity of a kind," according to Henry David Thoreau. You have developed a project that will help your students meet educational standards. But, you won't find just one opportunity to make the project you developed a reality. There are numerous grants that will offer you that opportunity. The important point at this part of your journey is the selection of the right grant opportunity for your proposal.

To implement your project, you'll require funding. Grants offer such funding, but you'll need to match your proposal to the right grant. The first step in this process is to go back to your worksheets and review the basics of your project. Focus on its subject matter, the amount of funding needed to implement your proposal and when you need the money. If your subject involves developing a classroom reading program, you won't want to seek funding from a foundation that gives grants for the creation of recycling programs. You should also consider the amount of money you will need when reviewing possible grants. If your program will cost $2,000, you may not want to seek funding from a grant entity that gives only $500 mini-grants unless you can obtain additional funding from other sources. If such additional funding is possible, it is likely that such information will need to be given to the mini-grant entity. In addition, you should think about when you need the money to begin your program. You may be trying to get funding for a science fair you want to hold during the spring semester. However, the grant you are researching won't make its award until June so it won't be an appropriate source of funding.

Finally, remember your grant application is simply an opportunity to seek funding from the grant entity. You may be awarded the grant, and you might not. Nothing is certain, so don't rely on the grant award until you actually win it. Don't be discouraged. If your first attempt at a match doesn't work, apply to another grant entity. Before you begin the process again, contact the grant giver that declined your proposal and ask for suggestions for improvement. Perhaps you needed a more detailed "needs" section or your budget may have indicated you were calculating your costs incorrectly. Some grant entities will issue the unsuccessful applicant a letter containing this information. If not, write, call or email the grant giver and inquire as to why your application was denied. Go back to your *Granted!* notebook, record those changes, and revise worksheets and other data accordingly.

Your efforts to find the right grant to match with your proposal will result in the gathering of lots of information about the grants for which you may wish to apply. Record this information on your "Grant Givers: Ideas and Comments" worksheet found in the Worksheet Appendix. Even if you don't actually apply for a grant from some of these entities, you will want to keep this worksheet for help on applying for future grants. So keep a worksheet handy in your *Granted!* notebook as you begin your "match game."

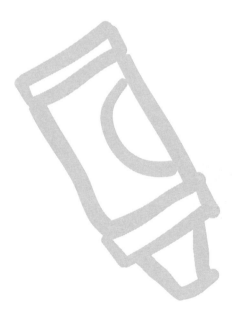

Here's a sample worksheet offered as an example of the kinds of information you will want to continue to gather.

## SAMPLE WORKSHEET: *Grant Givers: Ideas and Comments*

| Name of Possible Grant Giver | Type of Organization | Contact Information | Gives Teacher Grants | Subject Matter | Amount | Deadline | Comments |
|---|---|---|---|---|---|---|---|
| Rich Persons Family foundation | | www.rpfoundation.com rich@rpf.com Patti Pearson Exec. Director 111-555-5555 | NO – schools only | literacy | $1,000 | Feb 1 | Gave grant to my school last year |
| Large Store | For-profit corporation | Manager, Mary Merry 111-555-5555 | YES | classs room supplies | $100 | | Gives 2 grants per month |
| My School PTA | nonprofit | Paul Parent, PTA Pres. Note: He's also my room parent PTAPaul@123.net | YES, if teacher is a PTA member | professional development | $500 | Oct 5 | Gives 4 annually |
| Amanda Attorney | local lawyer | lawyer@me.com 111-555-5555 | NO formal grants given | | Met her at church & said she might pay for trophies for school geography bee | open | Call ASAP |

# ■ School Resources

You can find out about available grants from a variety of sources. The first place you may wish to begin is at your own school. Take notes of these conversations and place them in your *Granted!* notebook for future reference.

You may wish to talk with fellow teachers about their ideas for grants. You may find one of your colleagues has won a grant or knows another teacher who has won a grant award. These past grant winners will be important sources of information for you. They may lead you to some great grant resources. However, it is possible some grant entities may not want to award a grant to a teacher at the same school where a recent past winner also teaches. Thus, you may not want to apply to that grant giver even though your project is a perfect match. Fellow teachers may also have ideas regarding your proposal. They may have tried a similar project at another school or have additional ideas regarding how to support the educational standard in issue, so be sure to ask for the comments and advice of your colleagues.

Your school administration is another great source of information. Talk to your department chair, lead teacher and principal. They will know of grants your school has received in the past. They will also know of new grant opportunities since they often are recipients of newsletters and other communications that contain such information. This meeting with school administrators will be a good opportunity for you to determine the exact process your school requires concerning grant awards. For example, you will want to discover whether your school has any requirements that limit the ability of an individual teacher to seek a grant and to receive grant funds directly under his or her name. If your school or school district has these limitations, ask for and study any written guidelines. You will be required to follow them, so make those documents a part of your *Granted!* notebook.

You may belong to an education association. Such organizations are good places to find out about teacher grants. In fact, your group may even give grants to teachers for innovative projects to support classroom learning. Contact associations like the National Education Association, your state education or the New York State Association of Foreign Language Teachers, and talk to the staff about the grants that may be offered. They may also provide suggestions about finding other sources of funding for your project. Add the information to your notebook.

Don't forget to ask the parents of your students for help. There may be a parent who works for an organization that gives local grants or these parents may want to help you with your grant writing or research. In addition, many schools have Parent Teacher Associations or similar organizations. These local groups are usually very supportive of the teachers within their schools. They often have intense fundraising programs with the resulting monies to be used to improve the school in many different ways. You may wish to contact the president of your school's association to inquire about possible funding of your project. If they can't fund the entire proposal, they may be able to assist with part of it. In addition, parent volunteers through this group may be available to help with your project if such assistance is needed. If no funding is available, the PTA may be a great source of information about grants in general or local funding in particular. Your local PTA will be part of the state and national Parent Teacher Associations. These groups may also be sources of both information and grant funding. For example, the PTA of LaJolla High School in California offered grants of up to $350 to teachers for classroom or extracurricular activities/programs that would benefit the high school. Record the data in your notebook.

If you teach at a public or charter school, your school district and state department of education may have staff who can give you assistance. These governmental entities may also offer grants to schools and teachers. These grants may be given directly or through foundations created to support education within the area served by the district department. If you teach at a private school, check with the entity that oversees your school. For example, a diocese may give grants for educational purposes to the parochial schools within it.

## ■ Community Resources

There are often many sources of funding within your community. Take notes on what you find about such funding and put your notes in the *Granted!* notebook. Many local businesses and even individuals contribute directly to educational pursuits within their communities. Some want nothing in return while others appreciate some form of advertising of their contribution. For example, a local business may give money to buy new volleyball equipment for the high school girls' volleyball team in exchange for the hanging of a banner with information about the business in the gym during games. Be sure to check with your school administration regarding what sorts of such "advertising" are allowed before guaranteeing anything. Such funding does not usually require the paperwork needed in most grant entities' application processes. But, these informal transactions may still be thought of as "grants." Be sure to determine what would be required of you from the local entity and your school district if you accepted such funds. Of course, you will want to complete some of the post-grant activities described in Chapter Four, although the grant is informal in nature. For example, you may want to issue a press release about the grant and your project as well as evaluate the project's results.

In addition to small businesses and individuals who generously contribute to educational causes, your community might contain large corporations that routinely fund projects in the local areas or states in which they do business. For example, your town might have a manufacturing facility that is part of a large company that gives money for various charitable purposes. Think of all the businesses you patronize – banks, department stores, restaurant chains, grocery stores, etc. Their parent entities might offer grant opportunities on the national level, or the companies may give grants through their local store sites. For example, Macy's Department Stores through its Macy's Foundation has an "Earning For Learning" program that encourages employees, retirees and/or immediate family members to volunteer in their children's schools for 15 hours. The foundation then provides a grant of $250 per 15 hours, with a maximum annual grant of $500.

## ■ Internet Resources

Of course, many grant resources exist beyond what you might determine from sources within your school and community. You will find a wealth of such information on the Internet. It's a great place to extend your efforts to find the perfect grant match for your classroom project.

When searching online for an appropriate grant, begin by focusing on the details of both your status and your project. Your status involves your being a teacher of a certain subject or grade in a certain state. Your project involves a particular educational standard and a request for certain items or services. For example, you may be a high school math teacher in Oklahoma who is trying to get funding to purchase scientific calculators in your classroom to support mathematics standards. Open the Internet to your favorite search engine and type in a search for "grant mathematics teacher Oklahoma public schools scientific calculators."

You will have many "hits" that may or may not be helpful. Be sure to comb through them to determine what ones might be useful in finding the right grant for you.

Review the results of your search carefully. You may have discovered listings for organizations or individuals that provide grant writing services for a fee. You should also find listings of websites designed to support teachers specifically and provide links to grant entity websites that offer educational grants such as the one you are seeking. These websites may be supported by a variety of different entities. Many provide free information. If you are unsure about the legal status of, or other information about, any entity you discover online, do some further research. Contact such organizations as your state's office of the secretary of state, attorney general's office or similar agency.

Your initial search may also find sites that provide information on teachers from across the country who have won grants like the one you are seeking. This information may be in the form of an online newspaper article, a press release, a website entry from the grant entity, or the data may take a variety of other forms. When you read this information, you may get some ideas about entities you didn't know gave grants for projects like the one you propose.

In addition to websites that provide links and general information, your search will also uncover websites of organizations that actually give the type of grant you wish to win. You may want to review Chapter Two and the Grant Data worksheets in the Worksheet Appendix when you check out these sites in order to determine the type of organization offering the grant. You may find grant opportunities from foundations, nonprofits, governments, corporations and even individuals listed. Add information to the "Grant Givers" worksheet in your notebook.

Take some time to read through their sites and study the details of the grants offered. See what type of organization you are dealing with–foundation, corporation, nonprofit, government, etc. Does it actually give grants to teachers or schools? Most entities list the subject matter of their grants clearly on their websites. If you want to fund a reading project, you wouldn't seek a grant from a corporation that only funds science programs. What is the maximum amount given? What is the deadline for the application?

Your first searches were based on information on your status and your project. You may now have enough information to refine a search by limiting it to a single grant entity. Review the "Grant Givers" worksheet and enter the names of those entities into your favorite search engine, as well as the names of new entities you discovered that award teacher grants. For example, type in "grants" and the name of a corporation you know gives educational grants such as Target Corporation. You may be brought directly to the portion of the website that lists guidelines for the grant, or you may be brought to the grant entity's home page. If you are at the home page, you'll have to study the site to find the right place to click onto the grant information. Many entities list this part of their site with a term that includes the word "community," such as "community relations."

In another example, you may want to find out if Barnes and Noble, the book selling company, gives grants. Barnes and Noble, like many other corporations, has both a corporate website and a "products" website on which you can order items the corporation sells. With Barnes and Noble, go to the corporate website and not the site on which you can order books. You can find a link to the corporate site at the bottom of the bookstore's site. Once at the corporate site, go to "our company" and then click on "sponsorships and charitable donations" for the information you are seeking. There are additional links on that page as well. Keep searching and you'll find information about this company's corporate giving policy. It's not unusual to have to search and search to find the information you are seeking, but, the effort can be well worth the time. Repeat this effort for all the grant entities you discovered and entered on your worksheet that may offer teacher grants.

If you still haven't found a grant that matches your proposal, you may want to refine your search to find the most helpful websites to you. "Play" this match game by adding words and phrases that will focus your findings to the most appropriate sites. Search for grants for education, schools, teachers, educators, K-12 students, etc. Narrow your focus to charitable foundations or nonprofit corporations. Broaden your focus to charitable donations or grants in general. See what's being offered in your state or research nationwide grant offerings.

Your Internet searches will provide you with lots of data. As you look at these grant details, don't forget to list them on your worksheet, "Grant Givers: Ideas and Comments," found in the Worksheet Appendix. This worksheet suggests you list the name of the grant entity, its organizational type and its contact data. This data must be accurate and updated if necessary. You should note whether it gives teacher grants either directly to teachers or through their schools. If the grants aren't available to teachers, it is probably not the right grant for you. List the subject matter of the grant you are researching. Some are offered for any educational purpose, but others are given only for narrow purposes like to support arts education or to fund field trips. Be sure to list the maximum amount of the grant since this will impact your desire to seek an award. Finally, note the grant's deadline. Some grants are "open" and awarded several times a year. Others have specific, mandatory deadlines for grants issued only once a year. If you want to fund a project during your spring semester, you won't want to apply for a grant given in September for projects to be completed by February.

The "Grant Givers" worksheet records your efforts and helps you decide what grants to apply for. The worksheet should keep you from repeating your searches as well. You can better focus on the grants that match your proposal regarding its subject matter, funding amount and deadline. In addition to the worksheet, you may want to copy pages from the Internet that include such matters as grant givers' guidelines and application forms. Put them in the "Grant Data" section of your notebook.

Your hard work should pay off with your discovery of a grant that matches your proposal. You are now ready for the next phase of your grant journey. It's time to actually apply for that grant!

## The Paper Chase: *Grant Application Process*

You have now researched grants and found ones that match your proposal pursuant to their availability to teachers in the type of school in which you teach, as well as its subject matter and the amount of money you need for implementation. Choose the one with the deadline that gives you enough time to prepare your grant application package and makes its award within the time you need to begin your classroom project.

Grant entities may issue a "Request for Proposal," or RFP. These documents will provide much of the information you'll need to be certain the grant you've researched as a match for your proposal is, indeed, the one for which you should apply. Check with the grant entity for possible RFPs before you continue.

Some entities provide grants for projects that match your proposal but they require a Letter of Inquiry be written and submitted. Check the grant giver's requirements for such a letter. Follow these guidelines in your letter. In most cases it should be a page or less and include information about you and your school together with a description of your project. Set forth the amount of money you are seeking and how it fits into the mission of the grant giver. The grant entity will then notify you if additional information is needed and/or if you are invited to submit an entire grant application package. The Doris Duke Charitable Foundation is an example of a grant giver who accepts unsolicited Letters of Inquiry.

Not all grant givers require such a letter. In fact, if you are talking to someone with a small nonprofit or to an individual who gives funds for charitable causes, you may learn they need only an informal letter to determine whether or not they wish to fund a proposal. Other grant entities simply expect you to complete and submit their grant applications without an initial Letter of Inquiry. Thus, a call or email to the grant giver prior to the completion of a formal application for grant money is an important step in the grant journey.

Some grant applications are open only to those seeking funding after they register with the group online. The federal government requires such registration on its website, http://grants.gov. In this way, grant givers can screen applicants to be certain they qualify before the grant giver has to go through a review of their grant applications.

Record pre-application requirements you have completed. When you have finished such prerequisites for the grant you determined was appropriate for your proposal, you are now ready to begin the application process of your grant journey. But, before you apply for a grant award from that entity you should contact it if you haven't already done so. A letter, phone call or email inquiring into its grant program is a helpful step to take prior to actually writing your application.

When you contact the grant entity, speak to the person who coordinates its grant applications. If that person is unavailable, attempt to speak with his or her assistant. Introduce yourself and briefly tell the person about your proposal. Ask about the grant award process and be sure to record information about the contact person and the grant process in the "comments" portion of your "Grant Givers" worksheet. You may want to

Granted!

follow up on your application in the future, and establishing contact with someone working for the grant giver will be valuable.

## ■ Grant Application Packages

After you have determined it is appropriate to begin an actual grant application process, you will find they follow a variety of formats. Grant applications may be simple or complex based on the guidelines of the grant entity. Some will allow you to write a narrative of your proposal while others expect you to just "fill in the blanks" of the forms they provide. There are applications that must be completed online while there are also applications that will only be considered if they are mailed. As in every other part of the grant process, be sure to go to the source. Go to the grant entity and discover their application guidelines. Most entities have their procedures posted online on their websites, although you may call or write to see if those procedures can be mailed to you.

Go to your *Granted!* notebook and refer to your worksheets. Some grant applications must follow specific questions and formats written by the grant entity while others do not. Regardless of the requirements of your grant entity, the research and preparation you have worked so hard to complete will make your application process all the easier.

There is a wide variety of grant entities and, thus, a wide variety of grant applications. As previously mentioned, online registration is required for grants awarded by the federal government through http:// grants.gov website. After registration, qualified applicants complete and submit an application online. Many state and local governments require this online registration and application procedure. If you decide to apply to one of these entities, you may discover individuals are not allowed to apply for grants under their own names although public or nonprofit schools may be able to proceed with this online process. If you are applying under the name of your school, be sure you have permission to do so and follow all of your school rules, etc., in this regard.

You might find your project matches a grant offered by a smaller governmental agency or commission that provides funding to teachers for proposals that relate to the entity's mission. The application process for such a grant may be quite accessible and clear to follow. For example, the Hawaii State Foundation on Culture and the Arts offers grants through its Artists in the Schools (AITS) Program. The related application guidelines and forms direct you through every step of its grant process at its website, http://hawaii.gov/sfca.

As stated, grant application procedures vary widely. However, most grants for smaller sums designed for teachers' classroom projects are usually less complicated than the type of education grant a school district might apply for in order to support hundreds of thousands or even millions of dollars worth of programs and facilities. An example of a teacher grant program to fund smaller classroom projects is the Impact Grant Program of the Deer Valley Education Foundation in Arizona. This program supports educators in the Deer Valley Unified School District with annual awards of $500 given directly to winning teachers to support innovative projects that otherwise wouldn't be funded by the district. The application process for such grants involves the applicant's provision of basic information regarding their proposal and is found at its website, http://www.dvef.org.

## ■ Common Elements of Many Grant Applications

The two grant application examples have several elements in common. These common features are found in many of the applications you are considering for your project.

*In this regard, your grant application will probably include:*

1. Project description

2. Project need and/or goals

3. Project budget

4. Evaluation methodology

*In addition, your grant application may require you to provide information concerning:*

5. Connection between the subject matter of your proposal and the mission of the grant entity

6. Characteristics of your school

7. Characteristics of students impacted

8. Timeline of your project activities

9. Listing of any matching or supplementary funds

10. Approval by your school administration

# ■ Helpful Hints

As you write your grant application, consider the following matters presented to assist you in your efforts.

## 1. Be Sure You've Applied for the Right Grant

Applying for the right grant may seem like restating the obvious. However, grant entities often complain that individuals complete grant applications to compete for awards to fund projects outside their grant guidelines. For example, you might find a corporate grant that seems to fit your project perfectly. But, be sure you've done your research. You might find the "perfect" grant is actually offered only to teachers in the county where the corporation's corporate offices are located, and you live and teach in another county. You may discover another grant offered in your state and county that is designed to support projects like yours, but only public school teachers may apply and you teach at a private school. A third grant may seem to fit you and your project in every way until you call the grant entity for your initial contact and are told the grant covers only schools in which a majority of students qualify for the free school lunch program and yours does not. Obviously, you must always double and triple check to be certain the grant you are about to apply for is the right grant to fund your project.

## 2. Write to Address Your Reader

You have worked hard to present your ideas and passion within your grant application, but never forget to frame your presentation with the reader in mind. If you are applying for a grant from a professional organization, such as an association of mathematicians, be sure to emphasize the elements of your project that best relate to mathematicians. If you are trying to get an award from a charitable group in your community, you would want to emphasize the ways your project would benefit the community. Remember, people are going to read and evaluate your application, so keep them in mind when you write it.

## 3. Provide the Information Requested

Learn about the grant entity and its grant guidelines. Contact the grant giver before you begin the application process and ask questions regarding its work and its grant. If additional questions arise during the process, contact the entity again. Study the application form and any related documents. Provide everything requested, but don't provide what is not requested. If the guidelines state the application may not be over two pages, don't write three! If it requires a statement of matching funds from another entity, be sure you can acquire those matching funds and include that statement with your application. If the application is to be submitted online through the grant giver's website, don't email the application information on your own word-processed form. If it wants an original and five copies of your application, don't send four copies. Review what's required by your grant entity and provide it!

## 4. Take a Unique and Interesting Approach

Imagine you are working for a grant giver and you are assigned to evaluate grant applications. Once you have determined the application you are reviewing has met the basic requirements of the grant, what would you look for next? It is likely you would look for an innovative approach to the subject matter. As a grant seeker, taking a unique and interesting approach will make your application stand out. You are trying to help your students meet certain academic standards through your project. If that project presents a fresh approach to such a goal, the grant giver may feel more likely to fund such a project. This fresh approach should even apply to the title of your project. Make that title something interesting and memorable.

## 5. Focus on Your Students and Educational Standards

Most teacher grants should focus on student learning in general and educational standards in particular. Even if you are seeking funds for your own professional development, try to explain your need to be involved in that activity in terms of how it will support your students. Your focus on students will be much easier to show with projects involving classroom learning. However, it is always good to restate that focus within any grant application. Many applications require a statement regarding what educational standard or standards are being supported by your proposal. However, even if it doesn't, it is usually a good decision to explain such standards and how your project will work to assist your students' meeting of them.

## 6. Be Accurate and Thorough

If you are well prepared, it should be fairly easy for you to include only accurate information in your application, as well as to provide a thorough offering of data. Do not include any information in your grant application that is inaccurate. Accuracy is important in all elements of the application, especially the budget proposal. In addition, be sure your application is a thorough presentation of what is required by the grant entity.

## 7. Proofread, Revise and Repeat!

Don't forget the writing standards and techniques that apply to your own students' writing! Academic standards require students to follow a writing process that includes prewriting, drafting, revising, editing and publishing. In addition, their writing is to demonstrate the six traits of good writing: ideas/content, organization, voice, word choice, sentence fluency and conventions. Your grant application should follow these same standards. Be sure you proofread, revise and repeat! Then have someone you respect, such as a fellow teacher, do the same thing. You don't want to submit an application filled with typographical errors, poor grammar choices and other such writing problems.

## 8. Meet All Deadlines in a Timely Manner

If you win the grant you applied for, you will be following the timeline you prepared for the activities involved in your project. But, this "tip" for grant applications involves the meeting of deadlines established by your grant entity. For example, although some grants have "open" dates for submission, many have specific deadline dates. Don't lose out on a grant award because you submitted your application too late. Online grant submissions allow for easy to submit document submission, but your grant entity may require your application be mailed. You may have no real control over whether or not your application was actually mailed, such as when you use your school's mail system or through some other method that does not involve your direct mailing of your documents. However, regardless of the mailing process, be sure to follow through with a call to the grant entity to verify your application was received in a timely manner. There may also be other deadlines you must meet. Some grant givers require interim reports, matching funds statements, final reports and other such documents. You may jeopardize your funding if you do not turn these items in per their deadlines. If you can't meet these deadlines, be sure to contact the grant entity and ask them for more time. It will be the entity's call as to whether or not this extension of time is granted.

## 9. Communicate with Your Administration

Maintain communication with your school administration throughout the grant process. Some grants award funds to schools and not individuals. Thus, your administration will need to be involved in the grant process, especially regarding the deposit and expenditure of grant funds. In addition, you will probably need your principal's signature on your grant application to show his or her approval of your proposal. But don't stop there. Keep your administration advised of all aspects of the grant process, including the progress of your project should you be awarded a grant. Invite your administrators to your classroom to see your project at work. Discuss your findings and recommendations when the project is over. You may have to submit interim and/or final reports to your grant giver. Ask your principal to review the draft of these reports and get his or her signature as needed.

## 10. Communicate with Your Grant Entity

You should continue to communicate with your grant entity if any questions arise during the process. For example, you may discover that the company you were to order the workbooks that were part of your proposal from is no longer in business. You should try to find the same, or similar, workbooks from another company. Contact your grant entity and tell them of the situation, and ask if an amendment of your proposal/ budget is allowed to reflect this change. Communicate with your grant giver but, of course, you shouldn't make continual and unnecessary contacts.

# ■ Grant Application Checklist

You are ready to write your grant application. Your preparation is about to pay off! The worksheets you have completed for your *Granted!* notebook will be the framework on which you can build your proposal. Go to your *Granted!* notebook and organize your worksheets pursuant to the items required in your application. Review the worksheets and use the information contained in them to complete your application package.

The following checklist of what's needed to complete many grants may be used as a review of materials you have compiled and will now use to write your grant application. A copy is provided in the Worksheet Appendix.

| CHECKLIST OF GRANT MATERIALS | |
| --- | --- |
| _____ Educational Standards That Need Grant Support | _____ Evaluation Methodology |
| _____ Project Description | _____ Project Timeline |
| _____ Project Goals | _____ School and Student Data |
| _____ Project Budget | _____ Administrative Approval |

As you write each section of your grant application, refer to the worksheets you completed regarding the subject of that section. When you finish writing each section, make a copy of it and put it under the appropriate tab of your *Granted!* notebook.

## ■ Completed Application Documents

You found a grant giver that best matches your proposal, and you have completed its grant application package. You are ready to submit your grant application. Some applications are online templates that must be completed by the applicant by providing information on the computerized form and submitting it online. Others have application forms online but require submission be made by regular mail. You may also find a grant entity that will mail you their grant application package and allow for mail or hand delivery. Some may want only the original application documents, while others may want the original and several copies. As in many other matters in the grant process, follow the requirements of the grant entity.

Whether it was completed online, hand delivered or mailed, your application has been submitted. Make extra copies. Provide one to your school administration, and retain at least one for your own records. The *Granted!* notebook is a great place to keep your copy!

## ■ Grant Search Log

You have found the right grant match for your proposal and completed the grant entity's application process. Chapter Five introduces you to what happens after you have been awarded that grant. However, it may be possible that your application will be denied and you'll need to seek funding from another grant entity. In addition, you may win the grant but later have an idea for another project for which you'll apply for another grant.

You will want a record of your grant application activities for future reference. Thus, a worksheet, "Grant Search Log," is provided in the Worksheet Appendix for you to use in this regard. Keep your log handy in your *Granted!* notebook.  The following sample worksheet shows what such a "Grant Search Log" might look like.

## SAMPLE WORKSHEET: *Grant Search Log for Character Counts in Zombie Island*

| Grant Entity | Contact Data | Subject Matter | Maximum Amount | Deadlines | Submissions/Comments | Results |
|---|---|---|---|---|---|---|
| XYZ Foundation | AB See, Exec. Dir. | Grants to teachers for | $2500 Maximum | Application Dec 20 | Online application | Denial Received Dec 29 |
| | 111 N. Second | innovative classroom | | Final Report May 30 | Submission only | |
| | My Town, USA 00000 | projects | | | Submitted Dec 18 | |
| | 555-121-5555 | | | | | |
| | www.XYZ.org | | | | | |
| | | | | | | |
| 1234 Corporation | Connie Company | Mini-grants to | $1000 Maximum | Application: Jan15 | Application & 4 copies | Mailed Jan 12 |
| | Comm. Giving Chair | Elementary Schools | | Final Report: May 15 | to be mailed to | Grant awarded Jan 20 |
| | 1234 E. Fifth St. | for projects that | | | corporate office | |
| | Our Town, USA 00000 | support charter | | | | |
| | 000-000-0000 | education | | | | |
| | www.12340000.com | | | | | |

Granted!

# ■ Sample Grant Application Forms

Grant applications are as different as the entities that award them. For your information and reference, the following sample applications are provided to show you the types of documents you might be asked to submit.

**SAMPLE GRANT APPLICATION: *Short Narrative Form***

## Education Foundation Impact Grant Guidelines and Application

### Background
Education Foundation is a 501c3 nonprofit corporation whose mission is to foster excellence in education by funding programs that enhance the capabilities of Blackboard School District schools to stimulate students' academic achievement and enrich the learning environment.

Contributions to the Foundation allow its Board of Trustees to award grants up to $2,000 to individuals or groups desiring to expose District students to innovative programs, projects or activities that would otherwise go unfunded. Grants will be awarded to applicants facilitating programs or projects that expand upon traditional classroom instruction.

### Funding Criteria
All proposed grants or programs must meet the guidelines.

### Eligibility
Any District professional with a desire to enrich student learning experiences within the District is encouraged to apply. This includes Principals, Teachers, Counselors, Nurses, Media Specialists and all discipline areas.

### Each Grant proposal must
• adhere to the educational goals of the Blackboard School District and State Standards;
• align with and enhance the prescribed District Curriculum;
• supplement traditional learning experience through the innovative use of materials and/or activities;
• reflect sound pedagogy in both design and implementation;
• be intended for activities that cannot otherwise be paid for by the District or other source.

**Proposals will not be considered if the project can otherwise be paid for by the District or other source.**

### Selection Procedures
Applications will be reviewed by the Education Foundation Program Committee and Board, and perhaps the District's Education Services Department, to evaluate each proposal to verify that it aligns with state standards; agrees with the District's goals and prescribed curriculum; effectively supplements programs and activities already in place; is innovative and clear; and benefits students. Some weight will also be given to projects that will be of value beyond the year of funding.

**Final funding decisions will be made by the Education Foundation Board of Trustees.**

### Evaluation Procedures
Upon completion of the funded project, recipients are required to submit a written project summary and evaluation, including a budget expenditure report. Final reports for funded projects must be submitted to the Foundation within one month of project completion. Non-receipt of a final report will have a negative impact upon receiving further grants. **Original receipts and any unused funds must accompany the report.**

### Application Procedures
1. Answer all sections thoroughly, following the guidelines and criteria.
2. Submit application either online to foundationdirector@foundationdirector.com or in a folder marked with the applicant's name and school to the Foundation office which is located in the District office.
3. Funding requests will be presented to the Board of Trustees at the subsequent Board Meeting following the receipt of the proposal. The Board generally meets the second Wednesday of each month at the District office.

## Education Foundation Impact Grant Application

You may submit your application to Education Foundation via email or regular mail.
**Submit ONE ORIGINAL AND THREE COPIES**
The application is due in the Education Foundation office no later than
**4:30 p.m., October \_\_\_, _____ .**

**Amount requested** _____

Applicant: _____    Position: _____

Phone: _____    Email: _____

Project Title: _____    Project dates: _____

School involved: _____

Participant Grades/Ages: _____    Number of Students Impacted: _____

Subject Area/Emphasis of Project: _____

Will this grant supplement other funding? _____ (If yes, please explain additional funding.) _____

_____

_____

| | | | |
|---|---|---|---|
| _____ | _____ | _____ | _____ |
| Applicant's Signature | Date | Principal's Signature | Date |

## Impact Grant Content

1. Describe your project in detail. Include the educational/enrichment objective(s) and the need for this project.

_____

_____

2. How does this project align with District curriculum guidelines and State Standards?

_____

_____

3. How will you evaluate your project's success in achieving its objective(s)?

_____

_____

4. Describe the sequence of activities and associated time frames.

_____

_____

5. Provide a detailed budget and an itemized list of expenditures.

_____

_____

_____

_____

Granted!

# "BIG CORPORATION" and "BIG PROFESSIONAL ASSOCIATION"
## Classroom Technology Integration
## Grant Application Package

Application Deadline:
Round 1: November ____, _____
Round 2: March ____, _____

Administered by "Big Corporation" and "Big Professional Association"

**Classroom Technology Integration Grant Application**

### Introduction

Big Corporation has allocated to the Big Professional Association $200,000 through a Big Corporation Foundation for Education Grant to be awarded to PreK-12 teachers in the state where the headquarter of Big Corporation is located and who demonstrate an **innovative use** of technology with students. The funds will be disbursed to school districts, charter or private schools. The funds may be used to purchase the following for use in the classroom: supplies and materials, technology or professional development activities. Any non-disposable supplies and materials or capital objects purchased are the property of the district or school that is awarded the grant. Funds will be awarded two times during the school year. The first round will be awarded on December ____, _____. The second round will be awarded on April ____, _____. The funds must be spent by June ____, _____. **Deadline for the November Award: The application must be postmarked by November ___, _____. Deadline for the March Award: The application must be postmarked by March ____, _____.**

The purpose of this grant is to:

1. Recognize PreK-12 teachers who are using technology in innovative ways with students;
2. Increase an awareness of how teachers are using technology in the classroom;
3. Model best practices with technology integration improving student achievement.

### Timelines

1. Attend an informational session on grant procedures and answer questions at the Big Corporation Headquarters on October ____, _____ .
2. **Grant proposals must be postmarked by November ___, _____ or March ____, _____.** Proposals postmarked after that date will not be considered.
3. Grants can be applied for in the amounts of $2,500, $5,000 and $10,000
4. Grants will be awarded on December ___, _____ and April ____, _____, respectively.
5. Panel or poster session presentations of awarded projects in progress will be made on May ____ , _____ .
6. Presentation or poster presentation of awarded project outcomes will be made at one of the Big Professional Association's conferences during the year.

Eligibility

All certified PreK-12 school teachers are eligible to receive a maximum of one grant award. (This includes public, charter and private school certified preK-12 teachers.)
Applicants who are not selected for an award in December may reapply for the March submission deadline.

Technical Assistance

Big Professional Association Board Representatives and Chapter Officers are available to provide technical assistance and to answer questions. For assistance in applying for a Classroom Technology Integration Grant, contact the association by emailing bob@bigprofessionalassociationguy.com.

**Award Process**

Grants will be awarded through a competitive proposal process. All proposals will be read and judged by a statewide committee comprised of PreK-12 educators and business leaders. This panel will determine those applications that best meet the funding criteria using the rubric and scoring sheet included in this application package. The Big Professional Association will notify awardees in person at its biannual conferences held at the Big Corporation Conference Center in My Town, USA, on December _____, _____, and April _____, _____ . Award recipients not in attendance will receive notification by U.S. Postal Mail.

Required Videotaping

Educators who are awarded a Classroom Technology Integration Grant agree to participate in the creation of a digitally videotaped technology based lesson or showcase of the project. Educators who are awarded are required to supply proper student releases for videotaping permission. Big Corporation will digitize the video for purposes of sharing Best Teaching Practices via the World Wide Web. The digital video snippet will be posted on the Big Corporation and Big Professional Association websites.

Required Presentation

Educators who are awarded a Classroom Technology Integration Grant agree to participate in a panel or poster session on integrating technology in the classroom to other state PreK-12 educators at the Big and Important Technology Conference on June___, _____, showcasing the project.

Required Reports

The Big Professional Association will require from each awardee a report on the expenditure of funds as well as a narrative detailing how the goals of your project were met through this award. Guidelines and specific timeline will be provided to each participant awarded funds by the Classroom Technology Integration Grant Program.

Instructions

Each certified PreK-12 classroom educator in the state where Big Corporation's headquarters is located may apply for one grant and must complete all of the following steps.

Please review the following resources for guidance:
- State Educational Technology Standards (www. _____ .gov)
- Big Professional Association Technology Guide for Teachers and Students (www. _____ .com)
- See Appendix A – Proposal Scoring Rubric

**Step 1:** Complete the Classroom Technology Integration Grant Application Assurance Sheet included in this application package.

**Step 2:** Prepare a one-page narrative description of your project goals. Indicate clearly the learning and skill development that will occur for both the students and the teacher as a result of their participation in the project. (Use SMART Project Goals page included in this application package.)

**Step 3:** Prepare a one-page narrative description of how you will use technology with students in innovative ways, as aligned to the State Technology Standards. (Use "How You Will Use Technology with Students in Innovative Ways as Aligned to the State Technology Standards" page included in this application package.)

**Step 4:** Prepare a one-page narrative description of how your student-centered use of technology will impact student performance, as aligned to the State Academic and Technology Standards. (Use "How Your Student-Centered Use of Technology Will Impact Student Performance as Aligned to the State Academic and Technology Standards" page included in this application package.)

**Step 5:** Prepare a one-page budget narrative of what you are proposing to purchase and how this purchase will enhance your work with students. (Use "Budget Narrative" page included in this application package.)

**Step 6**: Prepare a proposed budget. (Use "Proposed Budget" page included in this application package.)

**Step 7:** Provide assurance of teacher certification.

**Step 8:** Assemble the proposal application and include **7 copies of each of the following, IN ADDITION to the SIGNED ORIGINAL,** in the order listed below, stapled upper left:
    **Page 1**: Assurance Sheet
    **Page 2**: Narrative Page - Project Goals
    **Page 3**: Narrative Page - How You Will Use Technology with Students in Innovative Ways as Aligned to the State Technology Standards
    **Page 4**: Narrative Page - How Your Student-Centered Use of Technology Will Impact Student Performance as Aligned to the State Academic and Technology Standards
    **Page 5**: Narrative Page – Budget Narrative
    **Page 6:** Proposed Budget
    **Page 7:** Proof of Teaching Certification Attachment
    **NO supplemental materials will be accepted. NO faxed applications will be accepted.**

**Step 9:** Submit the original and seven copies of your proposal via regular mail and one electronic copy of your proposal (e-mail or disk) postmarked on or before November _____, _____, or March _____, _____, respectively, to:

    Grant Guy, Big Professional Association President
    8888 W. 88th Ave.; My Town, USA 00000
    Tel: 000-555-0000; president@bigprofessionalassociationguy.com

## Classroom Technology Integration Grant Application - *Assurance Sheet*

Project Title: _____  Amount of Request: $_____

District Name: _____ County: _____

Name of Certified Teacher: _____

Name of School currently teaching at: _____

Address of School: _____

Years taught in K-12 public education: _____

Content area(s) that you are now teaching in K-12 public education:

_____

**I certify that if I receive a Classroom Technology Integration Grant –**
- **I agree to participate in the creation of a digitally videotaped technology based lesson or showcase of the project for the purposes of sharing best teaching practices.**
- **I will agree to participate in a panel or poster session on May 3, 2008, and to present at one Big Professional Association conference during the _____ school year.**
- **I will agree to submit a report on the expenditure of funds as well as a narrative detailing how the goals of my project were met through this award.**

| Superintendent Name | E-Mail | Telephone |
|---|---|---|
| Signature | | |
| Principal Name | E-Mail | Telephone |
| Signature | | |
| Teacher | E-Mail | Telephone |
| Signature | | |

## Project Goals & Activities

**TIP: Make sure the following points are clearly addressed in your narrative: (The goals should be bulleted and use the SMART goal format).**

1. What do you want students to know and be able to do by the end of your project?

2. What learning and/or insights will the teacher take from this project?

3. Describe the project activities that will support each goal.

## How Will the Teacher Use Technology with Students in Innovative Ways to Meet State Content and Technology Standards?

1. Is your project new and novel?

2. Are you pioneering a new approach?

3. Is it cutting edge?

**Possible ideas to incorporate into your project related to <u>teacher use</u> of technology:**

a. technology tools/equipment used in a new, innovative and/or novel manner?

b. novel instructional strategies?

c. new curriculum development and implementation?

d. multidisciplinary or interdepartmental participation?

e. involvement with the community or industry?

f. collaborative programs among students and teachers?

## How Will Your Student-Centered Use of Technology Increase Student Achievement?

**TIP: Make sure the following points are clearly addressed in your narrative:**

1. Is the project meaningful and worth your time to undertake to increase student achievement?

**Possible ideas to incorporate into your project related to <u>student-centered use</u>.**

a. project based learning?

b. student creativity?

c. self-directed learning?

d. higher order thinking skills?

e. inquiry and problem solving?

## Budget Narrative

**TIP: Things to consider while writing your narrative related to your expenditures:**

1. Relate each expenditure (in-kind included) back to the project goals and clearly provide a rationale.

2. Make sure expenditure costs are realistic.

3. Do your research; find out how much the technology costs.

4. Shop around and find fair prices *(Watch out for companies that charge too much for installation and shipping)*

5. Include any in-kind services/materials/equipment from your school/district. *(e.g. teacher time, equipment already in room, jump drives, CDs, professional development)*

6. Include only necessary items to implement the project. *(don't include paying teacher stipends (including yourself), travel costs and replacement items for years to come)*

## Classroom Technology Integration Grant Application – *Proposed Budget*

| Expenditure Description* | Amount Requested | In-Kind (not Reqiured) | Total |
|---|---|---|---|
| | | | |
| | | | |
| | | | |
| | | | |
| | | | |
| | | | |
| | | | |
| | | | |
| | | | |
| | | | |
| | | | |
| | | | |
| | | | |
| | | | |
| | | | |
| | | | |
| | | | |
| | | | |
| | | | |
| | | | |
| | | | |
| | | | |
| | | | |
| | | | |
| | | | |

Total Amount Requested:              $ _____

Total Amount In-Kind (not required)  $ _____

Total Project Cost                   $ _____

*Expenditure Description: Include name of item to be purchased, number of items and price per item, e.g. Field trip buses, 2 @ $100 ea.

**Add rows and edit categories in left column as needed.

Granted!

## Classroom Technology Integration Grant Application – *Proposal Scoring Rubic*

| Narrative Sections | 0 | 1 | 2 | 3 |
|---|---|---|---|---|
| **Project Goals and Activities** Prepare a one-page narrative description of your project goals and activities. Indicate clearly the learning and skill development that will occur for both the students and the teacher as a result of their participation in the project. | The project goals for students and teacher are not clearly stated and/or are not related to project activities. | The project goals for students and teacher are clearly stated but not related to project activities. | The project goals for students and teacher are somewhat clearly stated and related to the project activities. | The project goals for students and teacher are very clearly stated and related to the project activities. |
| **Teacher & Technology** Prepare a narrative description of how you will use technology with students in innovative ways, as aligned to the State Technology Standards. | The proposal does not address how the teacher will use technology with students in innovative ways, as aligned to State Content and Technology Standards. | The proposal provides minimal details regarding how the teacher will use technology with students in innovative ways, as aligned to State Content and Technology Standards. | The proposal provides some details describing how the teacher will use technology with students in innovative ways, as aligned to State Content and Technology Standards. | The proposal describes in thorough detail how the teacher will use technology with students in innovative ways, as aligned to the State Content and Technology Standards. |
| **Student & Technology** Prepare a narrative description of how your student-centered use of technology will impact student performance, as aligned to the State Academic and Technology Standards. | The proposal does not provide a narrative description outlining student-centered use of technology that will impact student performance, as aligned to the State Standards. | The proposal provides minimal details in a narrative description outlining student-centered use of technology that will impact student performance, as aligned to State Standards. | The proposal provides sufficient details in a narrative description outlining student-centered use of technology that will impact student performance, as aligned to the State Standards. | The proposal provides in thorough detail student-centered use of technology that will impact student performance, as aligned to the State Standards. |
| **Budget** Prepare a budget narrative of what you are proposing to purchase and how this purchase will enhance your work with students and correlate to proposed Expenditure Plan. | The budget narrative does not provide description of what you are proposing to purchase and how this purchase will enhance your work with students. | The budget narrative provides a minimal description of what you are proposing to purchase and how this purchase will enhance your work with students. | The budget narrative provides an adequate description of what you are proposing to purchase and how this purchase will enhance your work with students. | The budget narrative provides inthorough detail what you are proposing to purchase and how this purchase will enhance your work with students. |

# LOCAL GOVERNMENT GRANT GIVER
# GRANTS
## for PUBLIC and CHARTER SCHOOL TEACHERS

## Guidelines

We welcome applications from teachers in schools in our metropolitan area that are classified as public or charter under state law. We accept requests for funding between February 1 and October 1.

## Apply Online

You must first log in and register as a grant applicant. Your status as a public or charter school teacher within the metropolitan area will be verified. After verification, you will be emailed a code to be used to access the grant application process. Registered applicants may proceed to complete the online application using the templates provided. No other method of submission will be allowed. Only applications submitted through the online process will be considered for a grant award by the local government grant giver.

## Return to Your Grant Application

Log in to return to a grant application that you already started.

## ONLINE APPLICATION

### Government Grant Giver Grant

### For Teachers and Schools

**Primary Contact for this Funding Request:**

Prefix

Last Name

First Name

Middle Initial

Last Name

Title

School name and address

Please include your street address in the first line & if applicable, the
PO Box or Suite Number in the second

Type of School
e.g., public, private, charter

State

<Select One> ▲▼

ZIP Code

Please provide the complete 9 digit ZIP code (www.usps.com is
a helpful resource)

Direct Phone Number
Please use this format (xxx) xxx-xxxx

Fax Number
Please use this format (xxx) xxx-xxxx

E-mail Address

**School Primary Contact:**

(e.g., Principal, Head Master)
Prefix

First Name

Middle Intial

[                    ]

Last Name

[                    ]

Suffix

[          ]

Title

[                              ]

( Same Address as Org )

School name or P.O. Box

Please include your street address in the first line & if applicable, the
PO Box or Suite Number in the second

[                        ]

City

[                    ]

State

( <Select One>  ▲▼ )

ZIP Code

Please provide the complete 9 digit ZIP code (www.usps.com is
a helpful resource)

[          ]

Direct Phone Number
Please use this format (xxx) xxx-xxxx

[          ]

Fax Number
Please use this format (xxx) xxx-xxxx

[          ]

E-mail Address

[                    ]

## Proposal General Information:

Request Amount

[          ]

Project/Program Title
Please limit your response to 25 words or less

[          ⬆⬇]

Project/Program Start Date

( Month ⬆⬇ ) ( Day ⬆⬇ ) ( Year ⬆⬇ )

Project/Program End Date

( Month ⬆⬇ ) ( Day ⬆⬇ ) ( Year ⬆⬇ )

## Proposal Detail:

Please provide a summary of the project/program.

[          ⬆⬇]

Please describe how the project/program supports educational standards in the classroom.

[          ⬆⬇]

What are the ages and grades of program participants?

[          ]

What is the number of program participants?

[     ]

**Please indicate your best estimate of the percentage of those served by this project/program for each of the Ethnic Groups listed below.**

Please input whole numbers only (no decimals), do not input percentage signs, and ensure that your allocations total 100%

Asian or Pacific Islander

☐

Bi/Multi Racial

☐

Black or African American

☐

Latino or Hispanic

☐

Native American

☐

White or Caucasian

☐

Other Ethnic Group not specified above

☐

**Please indicate your best estimate of the percentage of those served by this project/program for each Gender listed below.**

Please input whole numbers only (no decimals), do not input percentage signs, and ensure that your allocations total 100%

Female

☐

Male

☐

Granted!

**Please indicate your best estimate of the percentage of those served by this project/program for each of the Diverse Populations listed below.**

Please input whole numbers only (no decimals), do not input percentage signs.

Disabled

[        ]

Economically Disadvantaged

[        ]

What are the anticipated outcomes of the project/program?
How will this program benefit the students served?

[                                    ▲▼]

What are the methods to be used to evaluate the project/program?

[                                    ▲▼]

[ Budgets ]

**Instructions:** Please complete the budget templates below. Please enter the detailed project/program budget. These templates must be completed exactly as they appear. Only applications with complete budget information will be considered.

[ PROJECT/PROGRAM BUDGET ]

| Income Sources | Current Fiscal Year ($) |
|---|---|
| School | |
| Government Grant Entity | |
| Other (please specify) | |
| Other (please specify) | |
| Other (please specify) | |
| Other (please specify) | |
| Other (please specify) | |
| TOTALS | |

| Expenses | |
|---|---|
| Staff Positions & Related Costs | |
| Consultant & Professional Fees | |
| Supplies | |
| Other (please specify) | |
| Other (please specify) | |
| Other (please specify) | |
| Other (please specify) | |
| TOTALS | |

Granted!

# CHAPTER FIVE:
# You've Gotten Your Grant, Now What?

Granted!

# Follow Your "Yellow Brick Road:"
## *From Grant Idea to*
## *Classroom Project*

In the *Wizard of Oz*, Dorothy was unsure about how to meet her goal of getting to the city of Oz and meeting the wizard. Glinda, the Good Witch, had some simple but very good advice for Dorothy. "It's always best to start at the beginning — and all you do is follow the Yellow Brick Road." As you start the final phase of the grant process, remember what the Good Witch had to say. You've started at the beginning, and now you must follow "the yellow brick road!"

You began your grant process by focusing on the educational standard you were having difficulty meeting in your classroom. You considered how you could help your students to meet that standard and what items or services would best serve those needs. You then wrote a proposed project that encompassed your classroom needs. You researched grants available to provide awards that would fund your project. You found the grant that best matched your proposal, followed its required procedures and deadlines and formally applied for the grant. You waited to hear the grant entity's decision, and you won! Congratulations! But what do you do next? Just take Glinda's advice and "follow the yellow brick road!" What is the path you must take to your goal of helping your students meet educational standards in your classroom? What is your "yellow brick road?"

You have won your grant award, and that's exciting. You put in time and effort to research and write it. Now you can't wait to spend the award money on the items or services you requested to help your students meet educational standards. To do this, you must follow the timeline and methodology you made part of your grant proposal. So, following your "yellow brick road" shouldn't be difficult because you've already paved it with your hard work.

Your past efforts and planning will make this phase of the grant process a smooth one. Author H. Stanley Judd said, "A good plan is like a road map: it shows the final destination and usually the best way to get there." Your grant application documents contain your plan, the road map to your destination. Your "yellow brick road" has been built. Now follow it, and you'll meet the goal of your grant, assisting your students in meeting educational standards through the innovative project you created.

Review the grant proposal and application data in your *Granted!* notebook. What is the standard you are trying to support? What is the project you designed to assist in this support? What are your project goals? What items or services are you going to purchase to implement your project? What is your timeline for accomplishing your goal? How will you evaluate your progress? What is involved in the Final Report? After you review your proposal for these basic elements, focus on what you need to do in the final phase of the grant writing process.

## ■ The Timeline

The first document to consider in this phase of the grant process is the timeline you created when writing your proposal. It may be used as a guideline for what is to be done and in what order these activities should be completed. The timeline may be enhanced by noting additional matters on it such as completion dates and informative comments. You may find the order and time of completion for your project may be different from what you originally proposed. Most grant entities know proposed timelines may differ from the actual dates and order of when individual events take place. However, deadlines established in the grant usually must be met. For example, the date the Final Report to the grant entity is due may be something that cannot be changed. If you have any concerns or questions, contact the grant entity to determine how to proceed.

Your grant has been awarded. You will now want to use the timeline in your proposal as an outline of how and when to proceed with your project. You can also use the timeline form to add information that may be useful to you when writing any final report required by your grant entity. Post your timeline in a convenient spot and refer to it often as you proceed with your project.

Granted!

# ■ Receipt of Grant Funds

You have been awarded your grant. The process of distributing the funds awarded under grant funds varies. If your "yellow brick road" was fully built at the proposal stage, you should be familiar with your grant entity's funding process. You may be given a check for the funds. The money may be deposited directly to a bank account. The entire amount of funding may be given to you or it may be given in stages pursuant to the details of the project being funded. Some grants reimburse the recipient for the purchases made in support of the project. Whatever method of distribution is used, the payment usually comes fairly soon after the announcement of the grant award.

Many grant entities distribute their funds in the form of a check. Before you cash that check and spend the grant money, several matters must be taken into consideration. To whom is that check issued? Is your name on it or is it the name of your school? When you were researching your grant entity you probably determined whether or not the grant would be awarded directly to you or to your school. Some entities give their funds directly to the teacher who has won the grant and issue the related check in his or her name. Others award their grant funds to schools, not teachers, since their rules require grant recipients to be public or nonprofit entities and not individuals. In addition, even if your name is on the check, your school may expect its teachers to submit grant awards to the school for deposit into a school account. Then it will issue a check/debit card payment from that account. This process may take time since these funds now have to go through a myriad of school and school district procedures before they may be spent. There may be purchase orders, invoices, receipts, etc., required, as well as selection of vendors from an approved list.

You may have already determined the procedure to spend such funds in the proposal phase of your grant. If so, review the process. If you didn't discover how to spend the money previously, determine the process by contacting your grant entity and your school now before the money is spent. Use the worksheet, "Distribution of Grant Funds," discussed in Chapter Two and located in the Worksheet Appendix to record this information. The following sample of this worksheet shows how it might be completed to indicate information about the manner of funding distribution for a grant to purchase books and school supplies.

Note: Deposit and distribution of funds in this sample form is more complicated because the grant money is not issued directly to the teacher. Instead, the school receives the funds and deposits them into one of its accounts. School and school district rules then apply regarding distribution of these funds and who the vendors will be. In the sample worksheet situation, these rules allow the issuing of a check to the teacher for her purchase of supplies directly from a local school supply store, as well as use of the school credit card to purchase books online from Five Star Publications, Inc. Both the store and Five Star may be used as vendors for the purchasing of items to be used in the school. The rules in this situation also require purchase orders to be written so a record will exist of the items to be bought, and the vendors will be notified of what will be purchased. After the items are actually purchased, a final receipt and notation of delivery are required to be filed with the school. This documentation will also become part of the Final Report of the teacher to the grant entity.

This process is more complicated than if the money was simply given directly to the teacher in his or her name. The need for the recording of the process of fund distribution in the example thus becomes more important because of the myriad of procedures to be followed. Remember that in our example situation, the money from the grant is the school's and not the teacher's. Additional rules of the school and school district will then apply. However, even if the funds are issued directly to the teacher, these rules may still apply.

## SAMPLE DISTRIBUTION OF GRANT FUNDS: *Mrs. Smith's Shakespeareans*

### Grant Entity

| | |
|---|---|
| Name: | State Arts Commission |
| Address: | 4444 N. Fourth St., Anywhere, USA 11111 |
| Phone/Fax: | 111/555-4444; 111/555-4440 |
| Email: | stateartscommission@USAstate.org |
| Contact Person: | Art Mann |

### Grant Funds

| | |
|---|---|
| Amount Requested: | $411.52 |
| Date of Application: | Nov. 22, 2_____ |
| Amount Received: | $411.52 |
| Date of Fund Receipt | Dec. 15, 2_____ |
| Method of Payment: | Check |
| Payment Issued to: | School |

### Deposit/Distribution of Funds

Check for $411.52 issued by State Arts Commission on Dec. 14, 2_____ and issued to

Neighborhood Middle School.

Received by Teacher, Sue Smith, from State Arts Commission on Dec. 15 and given to school

secretary, Ida Cash, for deposit on Dec. 16.

Purchase Orders issued by school to Five Star Publications and Anywhere, USA

School Supply Store for grant funded items, Dec. 20

Purchase Orders approved by XYZ School District, Dec. 23, & distributed by teacher.

School approval for use of school debit card by teacher for online purchases from

Five Star Publications and check cut for Supply Store purchases, Dec. 23.

Teacher orders project books using school debit card and buys project supplies using

school issued check, Dec. 24.

Receipts for Purchase of Project Materials

Teacher purchases/receives project supplies from Supply Store and receives receipt, Dec. 24.

Teacher orders/pays for project books from Five Star and receives receipt, Dec. 24, with books

delivered and received by teacher, Dec. 30.

Comments:

Receipts and purchase order submitted to the school on Jan. 6 and retained by teacher for inclusion

in Final Report.

Be sure your path along the "yellow brick road" is not littered with obstacles. Research the fund distribution process with your grant entity and school before you receive and distribute grant money.

## ■ Purchase and Receipt of Items and Services Pursuant to Your Budget

Now that you have received your funds and know the proper procedure regarding how to spend them, it's time to follow your "yellow brick road" on the way to purchasing the items and services you need for your project. You have already created a budget and determined where you will buy these items or procure these services and how much things will cost. Go to your *Granted!* notebook and review your budget materials.

Although you have already contacted them when preparing your proposed budget, touch base again with stores you want to purchase your items from, as well as the professionals you want to contract with for their services. It is possible that the availability and price of what you need for your project may have changed since you wrote your grant proposal. If their prices have changed or their availability is now limited, try to find the same items from another vendor or negotiate additional terms with your professional. Any such changes will require you to edit your grant budget. A small change shouldn't hinder you from the goals of your project, but a large change, such as the unavailability of the author of the book your class is to study, may. Contact your administration and fellow teachers for ideas on possible options. The grant entity must also be contacted regarding how to proceed if changes are needed. Be sure to record the outcomes of such contacts on your budget worksheet.

A budget worksheet, provided in the Worksheet Appendix, was the basis of the budget contained within your grant proposal. Review it and then enhance it pursuant to the actual purchasing of the items listed. You will need to provide some form of this information to grant entities that require a Final Report. In addition, keep all other documents, such as receipts, involved in purchases and contracts relating to your grant. These items may also be required to be a part of the Final Report to the grant entity.

See the following sample budget for Mrs. Smith's Shakespeareans project. It is a framework for documentation needed for the Final Report of the grant-winning teacher, Mrs. Smith. She will also attach all receipts for purchase of the items listed in her budget.

| BOOKS | | TOTAL | |
|---|---|---|---|
| Sixty-Minute Shakespeare Series by Cass Foster, $8.99 each | | | |
| *Hamlet*, paperback, ISBN 1877749400, 5 copies | $44.95 | | |
| *MacBeth*, paperback, ISBN 1877749419, 5 copies | $44.95 | | |
| *Twelfth Night*, paperback, ISBN 1877749397, 5 copies | $44.95 | | |
| *Romeo and Juliet*, paperback, ISBN 1877749389, 5 copies | $44.95 | | |
| *Much Ado About Nothing*, paperback, ISBN 1877749427, 5 copies | $44.95 | | |
| | | | |
| *Shakespeare: To Teach or Not To Teach* by Cass Foster | | | |
| and Lynn G. Johnson paperback, | | | |
| ISBN 1877749036, $29.95 each, 1 copy | $29.95 | | |
| | | | |
| SUBTOTAL | | $254.70 | |
| SHIPPING | | $10.00 | |
| TAX | | $17.37 | |
| | | | |
| SUPPLIES | | | |
| Tri-Fold Poster Board, $8.79 each, 5 boards | $43.95 | | |
| Tempera Paint, $3.79 each, 10 bottles | $37.90 | | |
| Brushes, 5 in packet, $3.79 each, 10 packets | $37.90 | | |
| | | | |
| SUBTOTAL | | $119.75 | |
| TAX | | $9.70 | |
| | | | |
| TOTAL FUNDS REQUESTED | | | $411.52 |
| | | | |
| | | | |
| | | | |

However, when Mrs. Smith went to actually purchase the items in her budget, she discovered the cost of supplies had changed. Thus, she first recorded the changes in her initial budget proposal and then prepared a final budget (see the sample worksheets right) showing the actual, final costs. She called her contact at her grant entity's office and she approved these changes. The revised budget with notations regarding the changes will be part of her Final Report.

## SAMPLE GRANT BUDGET: *Mrs. Smith's Shakespeareans*

| PROPOSED BUDGET | | | | Purchase & Receipt Data |
|---|---|---|---|---|
| BOOKS | | | | BOOKS |
| Sixty-Minute Shakespeare Series by Cass Foster, $8.99 each | | | | All books purchased on line from |
| Hamlet, paperback, ISBN 1877749400, 5 copies | $44.95 | | | Five Star Publications |
| MacBeth, paperback, ISBN 1877749419, 5 copies | $44.95 | | | Dec 23, receipt #333 |
| Twelfth Night, paperback, ISBN 1877749397, 5 copies | $44.95 | | | |
| Romeo and Juliet, paperback, ISBN 1877749389, 5 copies | $44.95 | | | All books delivered & received |
| Much Ado About Nothing, paperback, ISBN 1877749427, 5 copies | $44.95 | | | by teacher Dec 30, receipt #888 |
| | | | | |
| Shakespeare: To Teach or Not To Teach by Cass Foster | | | | |
| and Lynn G. Johnson paperback, | | | | |
| ISBN 1877749036, $29.95 each, 1 copy | $29.95 | | | |
| | | SUBTOTAL | $254.70 | |
| | | SHIPPING | 10.00 | |
| | | TAX | 17.37 | |
| | | TOTAL | | $271.44 |
| SUPPLIES | | | | SUPPLIES |
| Tri-Fold Poster Board, $8.79 each, 5 boards | $43.95 | | | All supplies purchased and received from |
| Tempera Paint, $3.79 each, 10 bottles | $37.90 | | | Anywhere, USA  School Supply Store |
| Brushes, 5 in packet, $3.79 each, 10 packets | $37.90 | | | |
| | | SUBTOTAL | $119.75 | |
| | | TAX | 9.70 | |
| | | TOTAL | | $139.45 |
| | | TOTAL FUNDS REQUESTED | $411.52 | |
| | | TOTAL FUNDS SPENT | | $411.52 |

Notes:    CHANGES BETWEEN ORIGINAL BUDGET AND PURCHASE/RECEIPT DATA

Original budget for supplies included $37.80 for brushes; new price of $1.79 per packet; saving $10  on original budget price; from $37.90

to $27.90, Dec. 23.    $10 savings spent on another poster board plus tax, School Supply Store, receipt #6789-1, Dec. 23.

Call to Art Mann, State Arts Commission, Dec. 23 -- approved change; to be noted on Final Report.

### Final Budget: *Mrs. Smith's Shakespeareans*

| BOOKS | | | |
|---|---|---|---|
| Sixty-Minute Shakespeare Series by Cass Foster, $8.99 each | | | |
| *Hamlet*, paperback, ISBN 1877749400, 5 copies | $44.95 | | |
| *MacBeth,* paperback, ISBN 1877749419, 5 copies | $44.95 | | |
| *Twelfth Night*, paperback, ISBN 1877749397, 5 copies | $44.95 | | |
| *Romeo and Juliet*, paperback, ISBN 1877749389, 5 copies | $44.95 | | |
| *Much Ado About Nothing*, paperback, ISBN 1877749427, 5 copies | $44.95 | | |
| | | | |
| *Shakespeare: To Teach or Not To Teach* by Cass Foster | | | |
| and Lynn G. Johnson paperback, | | | |
| ISBN 1877749036, $29.95 each, 1 copy | $29.95 | | |
| | | | |
| SUBTOTAL | | $254.70 | |
| SHIPPING | | $10.00 | |
| TAX | | $17.37 | |
| | | | |
| SUPPLIES | | | |
| Tri-Fold Poster Board, $8.79 each, 5 boards | $43.95 | | |
| Tempera Paint, $3.79 each, 10 bottles | $37.90 | | |
| Brushes, 5 in packet, $3.79 each, 10 packets | $37.90 | | |
| | | | |
| SUBTOTAL | | $119.75 | |
| TAX | | $9.70 | |
| | | | |
| TOTAL FUNDS REQUESTED | | | $411.52 |
| | | | |
| | | | |
| | | | |

Now that you have your funds in hand, remember to follow any distribution rules, contact your grant entity with any changes to your proposed budget, and create your final budget per the actual costs of your project pursuant to the format required by your grant entity.

As you purchase items or services, consider additional rules your school or school district may have in force. Some schools and school districts require purchase orders and/or other documentation be issued prior to the actual buying of any item, as well as the use of only approved vendors for such sales. Receipts and proof of delivery may also be required. You may need such documentation for both your school and your Final Report to the grant entity.

Once your project materials have been purchased, you should remember from your pre-grant research these items may or may not belong to you. Again, contact your school and the grant entity if you aren't certain. If the grant was awarded to your school, the items will probably belong to the school. You won't be able to take them with you if you leave your employment with that institution. However, even if the grant funds came in the form of a check to you, the purchased items may still belong to the school due to the nature of the grant requirements or school regulations. Place your additional documentation and final budget in the *Granted!* notebook.

## ■ Communicate with Others about Your Grant

After purchasing your grant items, follow your timeline with regard to what's next on your "yellow brick road." One of the most important actions you should take is to communicate your appreciation to the grant awarding entity. It is surprising that many grant recipients never thank the entities that award them grants. It is simple courtesy. The following sample "Letter of Appreciation" is based on a worksheet found in the Worksheet Appendix and is offered to help you formulate your own letter. Put your copy into your notebook.

Larry Learning
Big Town High School
678 N. South St.
Big Town, USA 00000

January 22, _____

Genny Rouse, Director
ABC Education Foundation
789 S. North St.
Big Town, USA 00000

Dear Ms. Rouse:

Thank you for the generous award of a grant in the amount of $2,000 made by ABC Education Foundation to the Theater Department at Big Town High School.

As you know, BTHS theater classes are filled with eager and hard working students. However, they were having difficulty meeting our district academic standards for theater arts inasmuch as our program lacked funding to present a play. A production would involve our students in acting, directing and producing, as well as technical and collaborative skills set forth in the standards.

With the generous support of ABC Education Foundation, the theater department will be able to present the play "High School Drama" during our spring semester. With this effort, our students will be able to be involved in the activities required of them pursuant to district standards. In addition, they will have means to demonstrate their talents and work to the community.

To express our gratitude, we invite you and members of the Foundation Board of Directors to attend opening night of "High School Drama" and a reception which will follow the play. The event will begin at 7 p.m., March 15, in the BTHS Auditorium. Please contact me regarding whether or not you and board members will be able to attend.

Thank you again for your kind and generous support.

Sincerely,


Larry Learning
Theater Arts Teacher

Many grant recipients meet with individuals connected with their school concerning the project at this point of the grant process. Perhaps you will meet with the school administrator to inform them of the status of your project. You may also want to let your fellow teachers know you have received the grant and are beginning the project you discussed with them earlier. If your project involves the need for parent participation, such as the holding of a science fair or the publishing of student-written books, this is a great time to invite parents to the classroom to discuss the grant and seek volunteers to assist you. Of course, the most important people to introduce the grant project to are your students!

## ■ Introduction of the Project to Your Students

A key to the success of your project is the enthusiasm your students show toward it. One way to encourage this enthusiasm is to make your students feel a part of the project as soon as possible. Once you have purchased the items that will be part of the project, you may want to bring them into the class. For example, if you have purchased books or microscopes or a laptop with your grant funds, show your students what you have purchased and tell them about the grant process that allowed you to buy them. If your grant involves the services of a professional, such as an artist-in-residence, tell your students about that person prior to the beginning of the project. You may wish to invite parent volunteers, fellow teachers and school administrators into your classroom to be a part of the discussion with your students. This also presents a great opportunity for students to write thank you notes to the grant entity to show their appreciation for the funding of a project that will enhance their learning.

Tell the students they are the most important part of your grant project. Describe the project to them and allow them to ask lots of questions. Be sure they understand the project is all about their learning a particular skill or gaining particular knowledge pursuant to educational standards. Their comments should be recorded and become part of your project evaluation methodology. You may want to formalize this process by surveying your class. If appropriate, pre-testing students on the subject matter of the project may be another evaluation technique. Place the data into your *Granted!* notebook.

# Pre-Project Evaluations

Interviews, surveys and testing scheduled for completion prior to the beginning of project activities should now begin. Your grant application may have included comparisons of various matters before and after the project. For example, if your project involves character issues, such as bullying, you may have decided to survey your students about problems they have encountered in this area and methods that currently exist to assist them in solving these problems. You would then survey them again at the end of the project regarding what they learned that is new and helpful. Finally, you would compare the results of the two surveys regarding how your students handle the problem of bullying before the project began and after the project is completed. Your grant application may have stated your intention to pretest your students. Your project may involve the purchase of history workbooks to support social studies standards. You may want to test your students' competencies concerning those standards before and after the completion of the grant-funded project. The results of the evaluation will then be recorded in any required Final Report and should also become part of your notebook.

# Your Project Begins

Your "yellow brick road" has now led you to the outskirts of Oz! You are about to embark on the project that was the innovation that impressed the grant entity so much it awarded you the honor of receiving a grant. Your items have been purchased and your professional contracted. You met with your administration, teachers and students. You have completed any pre-project evaluations. Your project now begins!

Your observations regarding the process, your students' reactions, etc., will make a great record of the impact of your project. Add any such record to your *Granted!* notebook for possible inclusion as part of the "recommendations for the future" section of your Final Report.

# Tell the Community about the Project and Your Grant Award

The decrease in per pupil expenditures by government sources described in Chapter One and the increase in the money teachers spend out of their own pockets for their students clearly show the need for nontraditional funding for projects that will support educational standards mandated by various educational agencies. Grant awards help to bridge the gap between what is needed in the classroom and what is actually funded. The larger community doesn't always know about the need for, and the awarding of, grants to fund needed classroom activities. Thus, it is important to provide information about your grant to the public. This information will educate the public about grants and, perhaps, inspire them to assist grant entities in their fundraising efforts. In addition, your efforts to obtain the grant and the hard work of your students to complete the grant project should be highlighted within the community.

One of the best ways to get information about your grant to the community is to have local newspapers and school/PTA newsletters write articles about it. Your school or PTA may have someone who writes press releases about school activities. If so, be sure to provide them with information about your grant and ask them to write and distribute a press release. If no one is available to do this, write your own release. Put it in your *Granted!* notebook and note where, when and to whom it was distributed.

Press releases can take various forms. The following sample release is based on the worksheet format in the Worksheet Appendix. You will want to create one about your grant and project. The release should contain contact information for the newspaper to use if necessary. This data may be about you or your school's or district's press person. Of course, you will include information about your project, as well as information about the grant entity. You will be telling the community about the work of your grant entity and how it might become part of that or similar efforts. Quotations and photographs are good additions to the press release. If you provide any information that contains names of students, be sure their parents authorize such publication. Send your release to local newspapers that cover school activities, as well as to your school, PTA and school district newsletters. Don't forget online local and school news sources as well. If your release is distributed during or after the project, you'll have the opportunity to include information about the work of your students and a photograph of them performing such work.

FOR IMMEDIATE RELEASE
Contact: Jane Doe, Teacher
Neighborhood Elementary School
123 Main St.
Anywhere, USA
Phone: 111-555-1234
**janedoe@nes.xyz.edu**

Author Michael Moorehead Visits Neighborhood Elementary School Thanks to XYZ Foundation Grant Program. High -res photos available.

### NEIGHBORHOOD ELEMENTARY TEACHER AWARDED XYZ FOUNDATION GRANT

Anywhere, USA – January 23, 2_____ -- The XYZ Education Foundation serves the students and educators of the XYZ Unified School District through the awarding of grants and scholarships. During its January 20 meeting, Mary Smith, Executive Director of the Foundation, announced Jane Doe, fourth-grade teacher at Neighborhood Elementary School, as the recipient of an Impact Grant from the organization. These $1,000 grants go directly to teachers within the school district for work on projects to enhance student learning and support state educational standards.

The grant money will fund a project entitled "Character Counts on Zombie Island!" Zombie Island refers to a children's book, *The Student From Zombie Island*, by 12-year-old author Michael Moorehead from Tempe, Arizona. The story is a humorous look at the way rumors about a new student can grow quickly out of control. Such a problem is one addressed in the Character Counts curriculum taught in classrooms, including Ms. Doe's fourth-grade class at Neighborhood Elementary. The teacher adds, "Children are to learn how to communicate care and acceptance of others, and I think the Zombie Island project will help us do just that."

XYZ Foundation funds will allow Ms. Doe to purchase copies of *Zombie Island* so students in her class will be able to read and report on the book and its message. Then the students and their parents will be invited to hear its young author speak at an assembly of the school's fourth grade. Michael Moorehead will continue to stress the good character themes of his book. In addition, he will talk to the students about his own experiences as an author and what it means to be able to achieve a dream, even at a young age.

The XYZ Education Foundation is a nonprofit organization founded in 1986 and was one of the first educational foundations in the state. The group's mission is to fund programs that enrich the educational environment of the students and teachers in the XYZ Unified School District through teacher grants and student scholarships. It holds various fundraising events throughout the year to support its efforts. Contact the organization at 111-555-1111 if you are interested in helping the foundation with its important work.

-- END –

Another method of communicating information about your project and the work of your grant giver, which may have been made a part of your proposal, is a reception or related activity. The sample Letter of Appreciation contained an invitation to the grant entity to such an event. Whether in this letter or through a formal invitation, it is always nice to ask some of the officials from the grant entity to your school to meet your students and see how their funds are working in the classroom regardless of whether or not an actual reception is held. For example, if your grant is funding a science fair, ask the directors of the foundation that funded the project to come and see the students' work. You may want parents and school administrators to attend as well. This may also lend itself to an invitation to the local press to cover such an event. Both your students and the grant officials will probably welcome the publicity. The students will be proud of their accomplishments and the grant entity may be helped with future fundraising through an article in the local paper. Note: Check with your administration regarding privacy rules if students are to be named in said article.

If the activity is to be an organized affair, an invitation may be required. Any sort of event should be coordinated with your administration. In addition, this may be a good time to ask your parent volunteers to help, especially if a reception with refreshments is to be held. The following is a sample of an invitation to a poetry reading and book signing that was the culmination of the work of fourth-grade students to study poetry as a literary form, to write their own poems and to publish their work through Five Star Publications' Kids Can Publish University. Note both the students and the foundation that funded the project are to be honored.

You are invited to a

POETRY READING AND BOOK SIGNING

to honor

the students of Mr. Sandburg's fourth grade

and XYZ Education Foundation regarding the publication of

*SANDBURG'S STARS,*

a book of poetry and inspiration


Date: Monday, April 9

Time: 1 p.m.

Place: Mr. Sandburg's Classroom, A-456

Frost Elementary School

123 N. Dickinson Road

Whitman, USA


RSVP: Mr. Sandburg @ 000-000-0000

We hope to see you at this celebration of the publication of the students' book of poetry,

which was made possible through the generosity of XYZ Education Foundation.

Even if a reception or other activity is not held, you may consider having your students write their thanks to the grant entity for its funding of the project in which they participated.

# ■ Project Evaluation

Your efforts were rewarded, your project completed, and now it's time to see if your "yellow brick road" did, indeed, take you to your destination. You set out to help your students meet educational standards mandated in the classroom and you established specific goals for your project. The evaluation methodology you included in your proposal will now be completed to determine project outcomes pursuant to your goals and standards.

The process described in your grant application must now be followed. You may be using one or more evaluation methods such as surveys, interviews, testing, observation of student involvement, teamwork, student reports and presentations, as well as a statement of key findings and recommendations. Your analysis of the data procured by various methods of evaluation may be both quantitative and qualitative in nature. There are many evaluation methods you can use to determine whether or not your project supported the educational standard you wanted it to. These methods should be established in your application and be administered per your timeline.

Review worksheets and the related grant application section placed in your *Granted!* notebook as you complete this part of the process. The Worksheet Appendix includes a worksheet, "Grant Evaluation Methodology," that is a good place to record your evaluation tools and related information. Following is a sample of this worksheet regarding a classroom project that involves a field trip to an art museum. The worksheet is a convenient place to keep the summary of the final data so it will be easy to refer to when preparing your Final Report.

## SAMPLE WORKSHEET: *Grant Evaluation Methodology*

| Date | Methodology | Results | Comments |
|------|-------------|---------|----------|
| February 14 | Observation Log | 50% of student scores below average on class participation | |
| February 20 | Test | 85% of students scored C or below on examination | Students told of grant & field trip & exhibited enhusiasm |
| Feb 27-Mar 5 | Observation Log | 90% of students scores above average on class participaion | Students highly animated at museum during field trip & after |
| March 6 | Test | 40% of students scored C or below | |
| March 7 | Key Findings/ Recommendations | Results Positive | Seek funds for future field trips earlier in school year |
| | | | |
| | | | |
| | | | |
| | | | |
| | | | |
| | | | |
| | | | |
| | | | |
| | | | |
| | | | |
| | | | |
| | | | |
| | | | |
| | | | |
| | | | |
| | | | |
| | | | |
| | | | |
| | | | |
| | | | |

## INTERVIEWS

You may have decided to interview fellow teachers and administrators before and after you formulate your proposal for their ideas and feedback. These interviews may be a part of a meeting with these individuals after your grant has been awarded. Parents may also be included in this process, especially if they are to take a role as volunteer assistants in your project. Conduct your interviews and record your findings.

## SURVEYS

Surveys may have been part of your evaluation process. For example, you may provide written inquiries for your students. These surveys should reflect the age and understanding of your students. Prior to the beginning of the project, you may survey your students regarding their ideas about the current curriculum offered to meet the mandated standard they are having difficulty meeting. After the completion of the project, they may be surveyed regarding their comments on the curriculum you have implemented through your project. They may reflect on how the project may or may not have helped them with meeting or exceeding that standard. Compare the results of your "before and after" surveys. Such a comparison may be useful for inclusion in your Final Report.

## TESTING

A part of your evaluation may be the comparison of past student test scores regarding the curriculum supporting the educational standard in issue with test scores on the subject after the project. This quantitative method easily lends itself to an analysis of whether the project increased student knowledge of the subject matter. Include your analysis in your Final Report.

## OBSERVATIONS

If observations are to be part of the evaluation of your project, you will find them simple, but often effective, methods of evaluation. You can determine much about the success of your project by observing such factors as the level of student involvement and teamwork during the process. These may then be compared with the behaviors of your students regarding the same subject matter prior to the project and its activities. Such observations may be qualitative in nature, but you can reduce your evaluations to quantitative form as in the previously provided worksheet, "Observation Log."

Granted! ◁▭◻)

## STUDENT REPORTS AND PRESENTATIONS

Your project may include your students' completion of written reports and classroom presentations. These activities, of course, involve lots of writing and analysis. Even if your educational standard does not involve the writing process, "writing across the curriculum" concepts would encourage student reports and presentations be made part of your grant project. Thus, you may have included the grading of these reports and presentations in the evaluation of the success of your project although the project itself does not support writing standards. In addition, a comparison of those grades to the scores on similar pre-project reports and presentations may be made within your evaluation scheme.

## ■ Key Findings and Recommendations

An evaluation of the grant project is required by most grant entities with results to be made part of the entity's Final Report process. You have used the methodology you described in your application. Now you should analyze that information. You may do this through a statement of "Key Findings and Recommendations." A worksheet to help you record this data is provided in the Worksheet Appendix with a sample of that data in Chapter Three.

"Key Findings" will be a list of data from your project evaluations that shows the outcomes of your project. To help you with your findings, review your "SMART Project Goals" worksheet. State your project evaluations found. For example, perhaps one of your goals was to create a school-wide public art project, and your "finding" was that 85% of the students in your school created wind chimes that were then hung in trees in the school courtyard. Another "key finding" might relate to a goal for the improvement of standardized test scores by students who participated in your project. The "finding" could be that a comparison of test scores from the last testing period to those after the grant project showed a 10% improvement by students involved in that project, while non-project students' scores showed no change. Remember the findings could indicate your project did not support your goals in the way you initially envisioned pursuant to your statement of expected outcomes. Positive and negative findings must be reported. For example, you could have established a project goal of improved student classroom participation through your project. However, your "Observation Log" may show there was no such improvement.

Analyze your "key findings" and then make "recommendations" for the future of your project and the use of items purchased through your grant award. If your project was successful, you will want to recommend you continue to offer it to future students. In addition, you may want to suggest fellow teachers incorporate the project into their curriculum. Even if your project will not continue, the items you purchased may continue to be used by future students. This use should be noted in your "recommendations." Most grant entities are eager to know the fruits of their grant funds will continue to help students in the future. Thus, even if your grant entity doesn't ask for such information in its Final Report, it is helpful to include such data on your project's outcomes and future use.

## ■ Administrative Review

As you prepare the data regarding your grant for inclusion in the Final Report, don't forget to meet with the appropriate member or members of your school administration. The administrators will want to know about the success of your project. You will want to discuss key findings and recommendations for its future. In addition, the school may need various documents regarding the grant for its files and possible submission to the school district or some other oversight entity.

## ■ Final Report

Grant entities usually require the timely filing of some form of a Final Report. What is expected in the document will depend on the guidelines of the grant entity. Review the initial grant application you submitted and any information it may contain regarding what is needed in such a report. Some grant entities may send you a printed form to complete prior to its due date. Others have their form online or simply provide a narrative of the kind of information they seek through this report. Some Final Reports are extensive reviews of your grant process while others may simply be a checklist that indicates what is to be prepared and mailed to the grant entity. Some require a formal, certified document and others allow for online submissions. Many times the more money you have been awarded, the more detailed is the Final Report. If you are in doubt about what form your Final Report is to take, contact your grant entity to assist you.

Most Final Reports will require a narrative about the implementation and outcomes of your funded project, as well as a detailed review of expenditures with documentation attached. Some grant givers want the school principal to sign the document. You should also provide your school a courtesy copy of the Final Report.

The first of the two following sample forms is a completed worksheet, "Final Report Inquiries," as the one from the Worksheet Appendix. It provides a record of information that may be used in your Final Report. The second sample form is based on a Final Report by an entity giving grants for field trips. Notice the bulk of the required information is to be added as an attachment to the form.

| SAMPLE WORKSHEET: *FINAL REPORT INQUIRIES* |
|---|
| Title of Grant:  **The Student from Zombie Island**! |
| Date of Funding:  March 18, 200? |
| **Provide information about the students who participated in your funded project:** |
| Total number:  850 |
| Minority students:  143 |
| Grade levels/ages:  75  K–6 grades/ ages 5–12 |
| Total number on free lunch program: |
| Gender:  males  51% ; females  49% |
| **Report your final budget.  Attach receipts to Final Report.** |
| Amount of funding originally approved          $ 1,026.40 |
| Amount expended                                              $ 1,026.40 |
| **If the amount approved differs from the amount expended, explain why.** |
| Note: Amount approved and expended was the same. However, shipping was not charged by |
| amazon.com for the purchase of copies of ***The Student from Zombie Island***. Thus, the resulting |
| $16.95 was used to buy a 31st copy of the book. Call was made to Z. Z. Zee, executive secretary |
| of grant entity, on March _____, _____, and he approved this change in budget. |

| Budget Item | Proposed Budget | Actual Amount Expended |
|---|---|---|
| 30 copies of | $15.95 each = $478.50 | $478.50 |
| ***The Student from Zombie Island*** | shipping = $16.95 | free shipping |
| by Michael Moorehead | tax = $30.14 | tax = $30.14 |
| | | additional copy purchased |
| | | $15.95 + $1 tax |
| Workshops by Michael and | | |
| Lynda Exley | $500 | $500 |
| | | |
| TOTAL | $1,026.40 | $1,026.40 |

■ **Provide information about any services funded through the grant such as work of an artist-in-residence.**

Name: Michael Moorehead    Contact information : www.ZombieIslandBooks.com

■ **Description of his/her services**

Michael Moorehead, author of *The Student from Zombie Island*, with assistance from his mother, Lynda, held workshops at Apple Elementary School on March 17. He performed a puppet show, read his book and talked about rumors to groups of students in grades K–3. He also read his book and talked about rumors, writing/publishing and following your dreams to groups of students in grades 4–6. Lynda and Michael led discussions with students about character issues concerning the telling of rumors and how to make new students feel part of their school community.

■ **Description of how those services assisted in meeting the goals of the project**

The theme of Zombie Island and its characters became the framework for a school-wide project regarding the harm caused by rumors and the need to welcome new students into the school. The project was initiated through the workshops held by Michael Moorehead and Lynda Exley.

■ **Describe funded project, including expected outcomes, as stated in your grant application**

*The Student from Zombie Island* was designed as a school-wide project to address character-related standards promoting trustworthiness, respect, responsibility, fairness, caring and citizenship with emphasis on addressing the promulgation of rumors at school and the exclusion of new students in much of campus life. The project would involve the purchase of 30 copies of *The Student from Zombie Island* for use and study by Apple School students. The book deals with the stated character-related themes in a humorous and meaningful way. In addition, the book's young author and his mother would hold workshops directed at various grade levels to discuss the book and its themes. It was anticipated that this effort would assist in dealing with Apple School's problems of the proliferation of negative rumors and the difficulty of new students becoming part of the school community.

■ **Describe the actual outcomes of the project**

As a result of the project, students began a dialogue about the harm of telling and repeating rumors, especially regarding new students, which resulted in open discussions, better understanding and the creation of a student welcome committee to greet new students and provide them with student "buddies"

Granted!

to help them transition into their new school environment.

**■ Summarize the methods you used to evaluate your project and the results**

The project was evaluated through student surveys and observation logs. The results showed 90% of participating students responded positively to the visiting author and related lessons and discussions. Eighty percent of students showed a high level of participation in the workshops compared to 60% levels of participation in non-project class work during the same time period.

**■ Provide the strengths and weaknesses of your project, including your analysis of items purchased through the grant**

The strengths of the project involved the high rate of participation and positive student feedback that led to the creation of a student committee that will continue to deal with the issues that presented the need for the project. The books purchased and the services contracted were an integral part of the project and its positive results. The weakness of the project concerned the fact that the 31 purchased books had to be shared by classrooms across campus. At least two more sets would have made the logistics of reading and studying the book a bit easier.

**■ What were the most important things your students learned through the project?**

The students of Apple Elementary School learned the harm that can come from spreading rumors, especially about new students. In addition, the project was created in such a way that students learned these character-related principles through their own efforts and not simply through teacher lectures.

**■ Submit photographs of activities funded by the grant for publication by grant entity**

Photographs taken during workshops will be attached to the Final Report.

**■ Describe your dissemination of information about the project**

Prior to its implementation, the school principal announced the project at the quarterly teachers' meeting. Discussions followed regarding project details. Parents were notified about the project and invited to attend the workshops and assist teachers as volunteers. A press release about the project, its grant funding and the author workshops was submitted to the school PTA newsletter and to the city's local newspaper. Both papers published the article with a photo, which will be attached to the Final Report. In addition, parents and grant entity officials were invited to the workshops and an assembly that concluded the day-long events. Grant officials were introduced and thanked at the assembly.

- **State your recommendations for future projects or activities using grant materials or data**

The project was so successful that its continuation is recommended. The "Welcome Committee" of student peers to greet new students and act as "buddies" for the new students' first semester at Apple School should continue. The books should rotate through the school with lessons created to promote character-related principles. If funding is not available to bring the author back to Apple School in the future, it is suggested the Zombie Island Curriculum Guide and DVD be purchased for use in future presentations.

---

| SAMPLE: *FINAL REPORT* |
|---|
| Association to Promote Education in Blackboard County<br>Field Trip Grant Program<br>**FINAL REPORT** |
| **NOTE: Failure to submit the Final Report may result in your school not receiving future grants.** |
| School or Organization Name: Chalk Middle School |
| School or Organization Street Address: 99999 10th Ave. |
| City: Your City, USA          ZIP Code: 00000 |
| County: Blackboard County |
| Phone # of School or Organization: (000) 555-0000 |
| School District Name: Abacus Unified School District |
| Applicant Name and Title: Debbie Desk, Seventh-grade Social Studies Teacher |
| Applicant's E-mail address: ddesk@chalkmiddleschool.com |
| Total # of Students Who Visited Museum: 88          Grade(s) of Students:  7th |
| Amount of Funding Received: $1,500 |
| Date of Field Trip: May 14, _____ |

**ASSESSMENT:**

Submit up to two typed pages describing the activities undertaken as part of the field trip. Include:

- description of field trip goals and measurable objectives
- concepts learned, how they were incorporated into existing school curriculum and how student knowledge was assessed
- previsit onsite and/or post-visit activities
- *State Learning Standards* met or supported
- list of partners and/or community resources used
- how funds were expended

**INCLUDE AS ATTACHMENTS:**

- all receipts documenting expenditures

- photographs of students during field trip

- student reports or artwork reflecting field trip

- completed Museum Field Trip Grant Program Evaluation Form

The **Final Report** and three copies are due no later than two weeks following your field trip date. Please mark your package FIELD TRIP FINAL REPORT and mail to:

**Harvey Homework, President**
**Association to Promote Education in Blackboard County**
**55555 Sixth Ave.**
**Your City, USA 00000**

**(Questions? 000/555/5555)**

You have followed the "yellow brick road" to your destination. You developed a project to help your students meet educational standards, and you wrote a grant that was awarded funding to make that project a reality. Your students have been enriched through your efforts. You should be proud of what you have accomplished! Your wishes for your students were *Granted!*

# CHAPTER SIX:
## We Won't Take You For "Granted!"

140

# Welcome to CafeGranted.com:
## *A Virtual Cafe of a Website for Grant Seekers*

You've begun your journey through the grant process by reading *Granted! A Teacher's Guide to Writing & Winning Grants*. You sifted through lots of information and discovered it is possible to fund those projects you know will help your students. Now you need some time to digest what you've learned and map out plans for writing your grant. You won't be left alone in the process. *Granted!* provides website support to continue to aid you along your grant writing and winning journey.

You've put in time and effort. So, it's now the perfect time to stop and relax with a visit to CafeGranted. It's a virtual café of a website that supports the *Granted!* book. Go online and log on to www.CafeGranted.com. Take off your shoes and have a latte or chai tea while you take a leisurely look at what's available to café goers.

When you come to CafeGranted.com, you'll find a great way to communicate about grants and the projects that they might fund. Chris Taylor, the author of *Granted!* blogs on the website. She uses her blog to highlight additional grant data and present more writing suggestions. Messages from fellow teachers regarding their grant experiences will be posted. A list of links to grant resources is available at the café. Samples of some of the worksheets found in *Granted!* will be found on the website, as well as a sample grant application package. You can order additional books on the café site and discover where the author will be speaking and presenting workshops.

Of course, no café should be without fun beverages and yummy treats, so CafeGranted.com even offers recipes for your enjoyment. A café is also a great place to hear interesting comments and observations, so Chris lists some famous (and infamous!) quotations on the site.

## Be Part of the Conversation

Stop by CafeGranted! and become part of the conversation.  Email Chris Taylor through the link on the café website.  Tell her stories of your own grant writing journey. Detail how the information you read in Granted! helped you in your efforts.  Share the celebration when you win your classroom grant!

At the CafeGranted.com website you will have a place to consider and expand on the information you have been given in the book, *Granted! A Teacher's Guide to Writing & Winning Grants* by Chris Taylor. You'll find:

- Chris' Blog, Cafe Conversations
- Links to Additional Grant Resources
- Messages and Testimonials from Fellow Teachers
- Information on *Granted!* workshops
- Online Store to Order *Granted!* and Related Merchandise
- Links to Five Star Publications and its classroom related books and services
- Fun Café Recipes
- Sayings to Quote around the Café Table
- Sample *Granted!* Worksheets
- Sample Grant Applications

## WE WON'T TAKE YOU FOR *Granted!*

CafeGranted.com is designed to continue the support and encouragement found on the pages of the *Granted!* book. You are encouraged to communicate your grant writing ideas, questions, and successes through the website.  To help you in this regard, the author's blog and educators' comments, as well as examples of *Granted!* worksheets and grant application packages are available on CafeGranted.com.  As you finish reading *Granted!* and begin to plan and write your own grant proposal, the additional sample grant applications provided on CafeGranted.com should be aid in your grant writing and winning journey.

## ■ A Sampling of the Following Granted! Worksheets Found in the Book Will Be Available at CafeGranted.com

### 1. Grant Data

WORKSHEET: Grant Givers: Ideas and Comments

WORKSHEET: Checklist of Grant Materials

WORKSHEET: Grant Submission Log

### 2. Educational Standards

WORKSHEET: Educational Standards That Need Grant Support

WORKSHEET: Statement of Need

WORKSHEET: SMART Project Goals

### 3 Project Description

WORKSHEET: What's Needed in the Classroom

WORKSHEET: Grant Proposal Data

WORKSHEET: School and Student Data

### 4. Budget

WORKSHEET: Proposed Grant Funding: Items/Services

WORKSHEET: Proposed Simple Budget for Grant Project

WORKSHEET: Budget Form

WORKSHEET: Grant Budget

WORKSHEET: Notes on Differences Between Proposed Budget & Actual Purchases

WORKSHEET: Final Budget

WORKSHEET: Distribution of Grant Funds

### 5. Evaluation Methodology

WORKSHEET: Student Survey

WORKSHEET: Observation Log

WORKSHEET: Test Comparison

WORKSHEET: Report/Presentation Rubric

WORKSHEET: Key Findings and Recommendations

WORKSHEET: Grant Evaluation Methodology

## 6. Timeline

WORKSHEET: Narrative Timeline: Sequence of Activities and Associated Timeframes

WORKSHEET: Table Format Project Timeline

WORKSHEET: Teacher Grant Timeline

WORKSHEET: Chart Format Project Timeline

## 7. Publicity and Outreach

WORKSHEET: Letter of Appreciation

WORKSHEET: Sample Press Release

WORKSHEET: End-of-Project Invitation

## 8. Final Reports

WORKSHEET: Final Report Inquiries

WORKSHEET: Final Report

## ■ A Sampling of the Following Grant Applications Found in the Book Will Be Available at CafeGranted.com

1. Sample of Online Application Package

2. Sample of Structured Application Package

3. Sample of Abbreviated Application Package

FIVE STAR ONLINE TEACHER & STUDENT SUPPORT

Chris Taylor and *Granted!* are part of the Five Star Publications family of books and services available to support you and work within your classroom, which includes Kids Can Publish University workshops taught by Lynda Exley, award-winning journalist and editor and co-author with Five Star Publications' Linda Radke of the book *Kids Can Publish!*

The Kids Can Publish workshop is designed to:

■ Excite students about writing.

■ Educate kids about real-life published child authors.

■ Get tips on how to get kids published.

■ Bring the nationally award-winning 12-year-old author of *The Student from Zombie Island* into the classroom via DVD to discuss writing, publishing and answer frequently asked questions.

The following sample grant application package highlights the possible classroom use of Five Star's Kids Can Publish University as part of a project to promote academic writing standards. In this project, the need to promote such writing standards is combined with the need to promote technology standards. Grant funding is sought so students can learn about the short story as literature, write their own stories, word process them into a printer friendly format and then publish them into a book that will be introduced at a book signing reception.

## SAMPLE GRANT APPLICATION

The following sample grant application seeks funding for the creation of a hypothetical  classroom project entitled, "Kids Can Publish."  It is offered to present you with a completed grant application so after you read it, you'll have the confidence to follow the steps presented in *Granted!* and begin to write your own grant. Read this grant application and then begin your own! As you continue this grant journey, remember CafeGranted.com is just a click away, and we won't take you for *Granted!*

## SAMPLE GRANT: *WRITING AND TECHNOLOGY PROJECT*

Project Title: Kids Can Publish!

Amount of Request: $1,620

Name of Certificated Teacher: Penn Sill

Name of School currently teaching at: Apple Elementary School

Address of School: 1234 W. Teacher Way, Apple, State 00000

Phone Number of School: 000-000-0000

Years taught in your state's K-12 public education: 5 years



Content area(s) that you are teaching in your state's K-12 public education:

Sixth-grade language arts and computer technology

School District Name: Apple Unified School District; County: Blackboard County

Number of Students Impacted: 30

Grades/Ages: Sixth grade/11- and 12-year-olds

Principal Name: Dr. Read Books

E-mail: readbooks@appleschool.org

Signature:

Date:

Teacher: Penn Sill

E-mail: pennsill@appleschool.org

Signature:

Date:

### PROJECT SUMMARY

Sixth-grade students at Apple Elementary School are a creative and hard working group, especially when it comes to their writing assignments and work with technology. The proposal "Kids Can Publish!" will incorporate these interests and enthusiasm for writing and technology into a project that will teach word processing skills while showcasing writing talents. Software designed for children's desktop publishing will be purchased and placed upon computers in the school's technology lab. Students will learn to use this software to create "printer worthy" copies of short stories they will write. These short stories will then be sent to a publisher for printing with each child in the class receiving a copy of the class's published short story collection.

# EDUCATIONAL STANDARDS SUPPORTED BY THE PROJECT

■ **State Educational Standard for Technology Productivity Tools**

Students use technology tools to enhance learning, to increase productivity and creativity and to construct technology-enhanced models, prepare publications and produce other creative works. Students will use formatting capabilities of technology tools for communication, including use of word processing editing tools to create and revise a document.

■ **State Educational Standard for Sixth Grade: Writing Process**

Concept 1: Prewriting
Prewriting includes using strategies to generate, plan and organize ideas for specific purposes.

Concept 2: Drafting
Drafting incorporates prewriting activities to create a first draft containing necessary elements for a specific purpose.

Concept 3: Revising
Revising includes evaluating and refining the rough draft for clarity and effectiveness. (Ask: Does this draft say what you want it to say?)

Concept 4: Editing
Editing includes proofreading and correcting the draft for conventions.

Concept 5: Publishing
Publishing includes formatting and presenting a final product for the intended audience.

■ **State Educational Standard for Sixth Grade: Writing Components**

Concept 1: Ideas and Content
Writing is clear and focused, holding the reader's attention throughout. Main ideas stand out and are developed by strong support and rich details. Purpose is accomplished.

Concept 2: Organization
Organization addresses the structure of the writing and integrates the central meaning and patterns that hold the piece together.

Concept 3: Voice
Voice will vary according to the type of writing, but should be appropriately formal or casual, distant or personal, depending on the audience and purpose

Concept 4: Word Choice
Word choice reflects the writer's use of specific words and phrases to convey the intended message and employs a variety of words that are functional and appropriate to the audience and purpose.

Concept 5: Sentence Fluency
Fluency addresses the rhythm and flow of language. Sentences are strong and varied in structure and length.

Concept 6: Conventions
Conventions address the mechanics of writing, including capitalization, punctuation, spelling, grammar and usage and paragraph breaks.

## PROJECT DESCRIPTION

**Describe the project's goals, activities, evaluation process and timeline.**

### ■ PROJECT GOALS

After completion of the "Kids Can Publish" Project, students should:

Be able to complete writing assignments using word processing software;

Be able to write a short story with application of the five concepts of the writing process: prewriting, drafting, revising, editing and publishing; and the six traits of good writing: ideas, organization, voice, sentence fluency, word choice and conventions.

### ■ PROJECT ACTIVITIES

Teacher Penn Sill teaches his sixth-grade students both computer and language arts. The activities involved in the "Kids Can Publish" project are based on the integration of these two subjects through the writing and publishing of a class-created book of the students' short stories.

Students will be introduced to word processing software designed for children that will be purchased through grant funding. Mr. Sill will demonstrate the software during the class's daily technology sessions in the school's computer lab. Students will then be allowed to practice these new skills in the lab. Mr. Sill will also be presenting the class materials on the short story as a literary form. In addition, he will be teaching the students how to incorporate the six traits of good writing (ideas, organization, voice, sentence fluency, word choice and conventions) when writing a short story. He will also explain the five concepts of the writing process (prewriting, drafting, revising, editing and publishing) to the class and how they will follow these concepts when writing their own short story.

After the students have learned word processing skills and are familiar with the short story form and the concepts and traits of good writing, they will begin to write their own short stories while in the computer lab under Mr. Sill's supervision and assistance. Students will discuss writing strategies and technology problems while in the classroom in preparation for their daily computer work. At the end of these sessions, each student will have written his or her own short story using word processing technology.

The students will then save their work on a disk, which will be submitted to Five Star Publications for publishing into an actual book! Five Star personnel will work with Mr. Sill as needed during the publication process.

Each child will receive a published book of his or her class's short story collection. These books will be distributed at a reception, which will be presented as a "book signing" event. Grant Foundation staff, parents, Five Star staff, fellow teachers and school administrators will be invited by the students. A Press Release will be issued regarding the grant and work of the Grant Foundation, as well as the details of the project.

## ■ EVALUATION PROCESS

Kids Can Publish! involves both technology and writing goals. Thus, the project's evaluation process will measure outcomes regarding both goals.

TECHNOLOGY GOAL

Students should be able to complete writing assignments using word processing software after completion of this project. The meeting of this goal will be measured by:

1.   Pretest of students' word processing skills in preparing a writing assignment
2.   Evaluation of the word processing aspect of the students' short story assignment

Grades will be assigned to both measures and compared by the teacher.

WRITING GOALS

After completion of the writing portion of the project, students should be able to successfully apply:
the five concepts of the writing process: prewriting, drafting, revising, editing and publishing; and
the six traits of good writing: ideas, organization, voice, sentence fluency, word
choice and conventions.

Prior to the project, students in Mr. Sill's sixth-grade class have been introduced to the concepts of the writing process and the traits of good writing as required by state academic standards. Their writing assignments were graded, in part, based on these principles. In addition, Mr. Sill reinforced these matters in sessions with the students during the project. They were encouraged to discuss ways to improve their writing using these concepts and traits.

The writing goals of the project may be evaluated by comparing:

1.   Measurements of student participation in classroom discussions concerning writing concepts and traits before and during the project.

2.   Grades of student writing assignments before the project and the grades of the short story assignment.

| Activity | Do What? | By Whom? | When? |
| --- | --- | --- | --- |
| 1. Grant Award | Foundation announces the award and sends check to school for deposit; Letter of Appreciation | Foundation, Teacher | March 4 |
| 2. Funds Deposited in School Account & Software Purchased | School Accounting Assistant deposits grant funds in school account and proceeds to work with teacher to order word processing software online | Principal's Office, Teacher | March 5 |
| 3. Software Received and Project Introduced to Students in Classroom | Software received and placed on computers in lab per contract; Discuss grant process and details of project with students | Teacher | March 10 |
| 4. Teacher demonstrates software; students begin working with software; observation of student involvement begins | Computer Lab work; maintain and begin work on Observation Logs | Students; Teacher | March 11 - 16 |
| 5. Test students on word processing skills; survey them on writing skills and learning methods | Students tested on software related skills; student surveyed regarding writing skills and learning methods prior to short story aspect of project | Students; Teacher | March 16 - 18 |
| 6. Teacher presents additional materials on writing process and traits, as well as information re: the short story in literature | Writing data presented with classroom discussion and suggestions encouraged re: publication element of project | Students; Teacher | March 19 – 24 (Students to develop story ideas during Spring Break.) |
| 7. Students begin to write their short stories per writing skills learned; software used | Students work on short stories in computer lab | Students; Teacher | April 5 - 15 |

| | | | |
|---|---|---|---|
| 8. Students discuss final ideas for their short stories; Short stories completed and put on CD; Teacher grades stories | Students finish stories and teacher records grades; CD prepared for Five Star's Kids Can Publish University | Students; Teacher | April 18 |
| 9. Observation Logs completed and graded: CD submitted to Five Star Publications' KPCU; Grant and Five Star staff, parents, fellow teachers, and administrators invited to project reception/ book signing; Press Release issued | Observation Logs grades recorded; CD sent to Five Star's KPCU with follow-up phone call; Students create invitation and teacher mails: Teacher and Principal issue Press Release to local papers | Students; Teacher | April 20 - 21 |
| 10. Books received from Five Star | Books delivered to school | Front Office; Teacher | May 21 |
| 11. Reception | Home Room Parents and students assist with reception/book signing to be attended by Grant Foundation and Five Star staff, parents, fellow teachers and administrators | Students; Parents; Teacher | May 23 |
| 12. Final Report preparation | Evaluation tools gathered; final outcomes/ recommendations prepared; receipts gathered; draft of report submitted to Principal for approval | Principal; Teacher | May 21 - 24 |
| 13. Final Report mailed to Grant Foundation | Final Report procedures of Grant Foundation reviewed and followed; original and two copies mailed through Front Office | Front Office; Teacher | May 25 |

## Project Budget

Itemize anticipated costs in the table below:

| Expenditure | Grant Funds | Other Contributions | Total |
|---|---|---|---|
| Software:<br>0000WP4Kids, Ltd.<br>www.0000WP4.com<br>Site License for School<br>Computer Lab | $599 | | $599 |
| Publication & Delivery of 30 Books:<br>Five Star Publications<br>fivestarpublications.com<br>P.O. Box 6698<br>Chandler, AZ 85246 | $920 | | |
| Teacher Participation | | School paid salary | NA |
| Reception Refreshments and Assistance | | Donated by parents | NA |
| Supplies: paper, invitations, CDs | | Donated by PTA | $50 |
| Totals | $1,619 | | $50 |

**Provide a brief description of how the funds will be used (100 words).**

A grant award of $1,619 would allow purchase of word processing software and publication of 30 books. 0000WP4Kids word processing software is designed for children who are learning this technology. The $599 cost involves the purchase of the software on CD, as well as a site license so the software can be installed on all 30 computers in the school's computer lab. For $920 Five Star Publications will publish 30 copies of the short story collection written by the students, as well as provide writing/publication assistance to the student writers.

# CHAPTER SEVEN:
## Worksheet Appendix

# Worksheet Appendix

The following worksheets were first presented in Chapter Two of *Granted!* They are organized by subject matter and indexed with black tabs. You may want to organize your *Granted!* notebook into tabbed sections named after these subjects. Then you can make copies of these worksheets and related materials and place them in your notebook under their appropriate sections.

Your *Granted!* notebook will then be a handy tool that organizes your grant data in a way that will be easy to find and work with as you proceed with your grant writing and winning journey.

## 1. Grant Data
WORKSHEET: Grant Givers: Ideas and Comments
WORKSHEET: Checklist of Grant Materials
WORKSHEET: Grant Submission Log

## 2. Educational Standards
WORKSHEET: Educational Standards That Need Grant Support
WORKSHEET: Statement of Need
WORKSHEET: SMART Project Goals

## 3 Project Description
WORKSHEET: What's Needed in the Classroom
WORKSHEET: Grant Proposal Data
WORKSHEET: School and Student Data

## 4. Budget
WORKSHEET: Proposed Grant Funding: Items/Services
WORKSHEET: Proposed Simple Budget for Grant Project
WORKSHEET: Budget Form
WORKSHEET: Grant Budget
WORKSHEET: Notes on Differences Between Proposed Budget & Actual Purchases
WORKSHEET: Final Budget
WORKSHEET: Distribution of Grant Funds

## 5. Evaluation Methodology
WORKSHEET: Student Survey
WORKSHEET: Observation Log
WORKSHEET: Test Comparison
WORKSHEET: Report/Presentation Rubric
WORKSHEET: Key Findings and Recommendations
WORKSHEET: Grant Evaluation Methodology

## 6. Timeline
WORKSHEET: Narrative Timeline: Sequence of Activities and Associated Timeframes
WORKSHEET: Table Format Project Timeline
WORKSHEET: Teacher Grant Timeline
WORKSHEET: Chart Format Project Timeline

## 7. Publicity and Outreach
WORKSHEET: Letter of Appreciation
WORKSHEET: Sample Press Release
WORKSHEET: End-of-Project Invitation

## 8. Final Reports
WORKSHEET: Final Report Inquiries
WORKSHEET: Final Report

## WORKSHEET GRANT GIVERS: *Ideas and Comments*

| Name of Possible Grant Giver | Type of Organization | Contact Information | Gives Teacher Grants | Subject Matter | Amount | Deadline | Comments |
|---|---|---|---|---|---|---|---|
| | | | | | | | |
| | | | | | | | |
| | | | | | | | |
| | | | | | | | |
| | | | | | | | |
| | | | | | | | |
| | | | | | | | |
| | | | | | | | |
| | | | | | | | |
| | | | | | | | |
| | | | | | | | |
| | | | | | | | |
| | | | | | | | |
| | | | | | | | |
| | | | | | | | |
| | | | | | | | |
| | | | | | | | |
| | | | | | | | |
| | | | | | | | |
| | | | | | | | |
| | | | | | | | |

## WORKSHEET: *Checklist of Grant Materials*

Granted!

———————  Educational Standards that Need Grant Support

———————  Project Description

———————  Project Goals

———————  Project Budget

———————  Evaluation Methodology

———————  Project Timeline

———————  School and Student Data

———————  Administrative Approval

WORKSHEET: *Grant Submission Log*

| Grant Entity | Contact Data | Subject Matter | Maximum Amount | Deadlines | Submissions/Comments | Results |
|---|---|---|---|---|---|---|
| | | | | | | |
| | | | | | | |
| | | | | | | |
| | | | | | | |
| | | | | | | |
| | | | | | | |
| | | | | | | |
| | | | | | | |
| | | | | | | |
| | | | | | | |
| | | | | | | |
| | | | | | | |
| | | | | | | |
| | | | | | | |
| | | | | | | |
| | | | | | | |
| | | | | | | |
| | | | | | | |
| | | | | | | |

## WORKSHEET: *Educational Standards That Need Grant Support*

Entity establishing the standard: _____

Web address: _____

What standard is difficult to meet within the classroom? _____

_____

_____

_____

_____

_____

_____

_____

Where may the standard be found? _____

_____

Summary of standard: _____

_____

_____

Why is that standard not being met? _____

_____

_____

Comments/Notes: Project would be great addition to creative writing sessions next semester. _____

_____

_____

_____

_____

_____

Granted! ✏️

State the academic standard your students are having difficulty meeting/exceeding and describe the evidence of that difficulty.

_____

_____

_____

_____

_____

_____

_____

_____

_____

_____

_____

_____

_____

_____

_____

_____

_____

_____

_____

_____

_____

_____

**EDUCATIONAL STANDARDS**

S (Specific Goals) _____

_____

_____

_____

_____

_____

M (Measurable) _____

_____

_____

_____

_____

A (Achievable) _____

_____

_____

_____

_____

R (Realistic) _____

_____

_____

_____

_____

T (Time-Bound) _____

_____

_____

_____

_____

**EDUCATIONAL STANDARDS**

Granted!

## WORKSHEET: *What's Needed in the Classroom*

**Educational Standard to be Supported:**

| Items Needed | Description/Quantity | Price Estimate | Where to Purchase |
|---|---|---|---|
| Books | | | |
| Supplies | | | |
| Equipment | | | |
| Computer/Hardware | | | |
| Computer Software | | | |
| Media (CD, DVD, etc.) | | | |
| Other | | | |
| Professional Services | | | |
| **Comments/Notes:** | | | |

1. Educational Standard: _____

_____

_____

_____

_____

_____

_____

_____

_____

2. Brief Description of Project: _____

_____

_____

_____

_____

_____

_____

_____

_____

3. Name of Project and Comments if Applicable: _____

_____

_____

_____

_____

_____

_____

_____

**PROJECT DESCRIPTION**

**SCHOOL DATA**

Name: _____

Address: _____

School District: _____

Fax: _____

Phone: _____

Website: _____

Principal: _____

Tax Number: _____

Type of Institution: _____

Grades Taught: _____

Number of Students: _____

Title I: _____

Diversity Statistics: _____

Other Information: _____

_____

_____

**STUDENT DATA** (regarding those to be involved in grant-funded project)

Grade(s): _____

Age(s): _____

Number Impacted by Grant Project: _____

Title I: _____

Diversity Statistics: _____

Other Information: _____

_____

_____

**PROJECT DESCRIPTION**

# BUDGET

## WORKSHEET: *Proposed Grant Funding: Items/Services*

| Items/Service | Description | Qty | Cost | | | | Vendor | Funding Source |
|---|---|---|---|---|---|---|---|---|
| | | | Each | Shipping | Tax | Total | | |
| Books | | | | | | | | |
| | | | | | | | | |
| | | | | | | | | |
| Supplies | | | | | | | | |
| | | | | | | | | |
| | | | | | | | | |
| Computer Equipment | | | | | | | | |
| | | | | | | | | |
| | | | | | | | | |
| Computer Software | | | | | | | | |
| | | | | | | | | |
| | | | | | | | | |
| Media | | | | | | | | |
| Other | | | | | | | | |
| Professional Services | | | | | | | | |
| | | | | | | | | |

## WORKSHEET: *Proposed Simple Budget*

| Funding Requested for Purchase of: | QTY | Price | Vendor |
|---|---|---|---|
| | | | |
| | | | |
| | | | |
| | | | |
| | | | |
| | | | |
| | | | |
| | | | |
| | | | |
| | | | |
| | | | |
| | | | |
| | | | |
| | | | |
| | | | |
| | | | |
| | | | |
| | | | |
| | | | |
| | | | |
| | | | |
| | | | |
| | | | |
| | | | |
| | | | |
| | | | |
| | | | |
| | | | |
| | | | |
| | | | |
| | | | |
| | | | |
| | Subtotal | | |
| | Tax | | |
| **Total Funds Requested** | | | |

BUDGET

## WORKSHEET: *Grant Budget*

| BOOKS | | TOTAL | |
|---|---|---|---|
| | | | |
| | | | |
| | | | |
| | | | |
| | | | |
| SUBTOTAL | | | |
| SHIPPING | | | |
| TAX | | | |
| | | | |
| SUPPLIES | | | |
| | | | |
| | | | |
| | | | |
| | | | |
| | | | |
| SUBTOTAL | | | |
| SHIPPING | | | |
| TAX | | | |
| | | | |
| TECHNOLOGY & MEDIA | | | |
| | | | |
| | | | |
| | | | |
| | | | |
| | | | |
| SUBTOTAL | | | |
| SHIPPING | | | |
| TAX | | | |
| | | | |
| CONTRACTED SERVICES | | | |
| | | | |
| | | | |
| | | | |
| | | | |
| SUBTOTAL | | | |
| SHIPPING | | | |
| TAX | | | |
| | | | |
| TOTAL FUNDS REQUESTED | | | |

Granted!

# WORKSHEET: *Notes on Differences between Proposed Budget & Purchases*

| PROPOSED BUDGET | | | | Purchase & Receipt Data | | | |
|---|---|---|---|---|---|---|---|
| BOOKS | | | | BOOKS | | | |
| | | | | | | | |
| | | | SUBTOTAL | | | | |
| | | | SHIPPING | | | | |
| | | | TAX | | | | |
| | | | TOTAL | | | | |
| SUPPLIES | | | | SUPPLIES | | | |
| | | | | | | | |
| | | | SUBTOTAL | | | | |
| | | | SHIPPING | | | | |
| | | | TAX | | | | |
| | | | TOTAL | | | | |
| TECHNOLOGY & MEDIA | | | | TECHNOLOGY & MEDIA | | | |
| | | | | | | | |
| | | | SUBTOTAL | | | | |
| | | | SHIPPING | | | | |
| | | | TAX | | | | |
| | | | TOTAL | | | | |
| CONTRACTED SERVICES | | | | CONTRACTED SERVICES | | | |
| | | | | | | | |
| | | | SUBTOTAL | | | | |
| | | | SHIPPING | | | | |
| | | | TAX | | | | |
| | | | TOTAL | | | | |
| | | | TOTAL FUNDS REQUESTED | | | | |
| | | | TOTAL FUNDS SPENT | | | | |

Notes:   CHANGES BETWEEN ORIGINAL BUDGET AND PURCHASE/RECEIPT DATA

 Granted!

## WORKSHEET: *FINAL BUDGET*

| BUDGET CATEGORY/EXPLANATION | AMOUNT | SUPPORTED BY |
|---|---|---|
| **Cash Expenses** | | |
| | $ | |
| | | |
| | | |
| | | |
| | | |
| | | |
| | | |
| | | |
| | | |
| | | |
| | | |
| | | |
| | | |
| | | |
| | | |
| | | |
| | | |
| | | |
| | | |
| | | |
| | | |
| | | |
| | | |
| | | |
| | $ | |
| | $ | |
| TOTAL CASH EXPENSES | $ | |
| **Cash Income** | | |
| | | |
| | $ | |
| | $ | |
| TOTAL CASH INCOME | $ | |
| **In-Kind Support** | | |
| | $ | |
| | $ | |
| TOTAL IN-KIND SUPPORT | $ | |
| **BUDGET SUMMARY** | | |
| Grant Request | $ | Amount requested from Grant Entity |
| Cash Match | $ | Cash Income not including grant funds |
| In-Kind Support | $ | Total donated services/materials |
| TOTAL PROJECT BUDGET | $ | Sum of above |

Granted!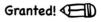

## WORKSHEET: *Distribution of Grant Funds*

**Grant Entity**

| | |
|---|---|
| | Name: |
| | Address: |
| | Phone/Fax: |
| | Email: |
| | Contact Person: |

**Grant Funds**

| | |
|---|---|
| | Amount Requested: |
| | Date of Application: |
| | Amount Received: |
| | Date of Fund Receipt |
| | Method of Payment: |
| | Payment Issued to: |

**Deposit/Distribution of Funds**

Receipts for Purchase of Project Materials

COMMENTS:

BUDGET

## WORKSHEET: *Student Survey*

Teacher: _____

Date: _____

Subject of Survey: _____

**Circle the number that is closest to how you feel about the statement. If you don't know or don't have an opinion, circle the X.**

5  Strongly Agree

4  Agree

3  Neutral (neither agree nor disagree)

1  Strongly Disagree

X  Don't know / No Opinion

| | Don't Know/ No Opinion | Strongly disagree | Disagree | Neutral | Agree | Strongly Agree |
|---|---|---|---|---|---|---|
| 1. | X | 1 | 2 | 3 | 4 | 5 |
| 2. | X | 1 | 2 | 3 | 4 | 5 |
| 3. | X | 1 | 2 | 3 | 4 | 5 |
| 4. | X | 1 | 2 | 3 | 4 | 5 |
| 5. | X | 1 | 2 | 3 | 4 | 5 |
| 6. | X | 1 | 2 | 3 | 4 | 5 |
| 7. | X | 1 | 2 | 3 | 4 | 5 |
| 8. | X | 1 | 2 | 3 | 4 | 5 |
| 9. | X | 1 | 2 | 3 | 4 | 5 |
| 10. | X | 1 | 2 | 3 | 4 | 5 |
| 11. | X | 1 | 2 | 3 | 4 | 5 |
| 12. | X | 1 | 2 | 3 | 4 | 5 |
| 13. | X | 1 | 2 | 3 | 4 | 5 |
| 14. | X | 1 | 2 | 3 | 4 | 5 |
| 15. | X | 1 | 2 | 3 | 4 | 5 |
| 16. | X | 1 | 2 | 3 | 4 | 5 |
| 17. | X | 1 | 2 | 3 | 4 | 5 |
| 18. | X | 1 | 2 | 3 | 4 | 5 |
| 19. | X | 1 | 2 | 3 | 4 | 5 |
| 20. | X | 1 | 2 | 3 | 4 | 5 |
| 21. | X | 1 | 2 | 3 | 4 | 5 |

**EVALUATION METHODOLOGY**

**Project:** _____

**Date:** _____

**Observation:** _____

_____

**Score Scale:**

  5  *Strongly Agree*

  4  *Agree*

  3  *Neutral (neither agree nor disagree)*

  2  *Disagree*

  1  *Strongly Disagree*

  X  *Student Absent*

| Student Name: | Score: | Comments: |
|---|---|---|
|  |  |  |
|  |  |  |
|  |  |  |
|  |  |  |
|  |  |  |
|  |  |  |
|  |  |  |
|  |  |  |
|  |  |  |
|  |  |  |
|  |  |  |
|  |  |  |
|  |  |  |
|  |  |  |
|  |  |  |
|  |  |  |
|  |  |  |
|  |  |  |
|  |  |  |

## WORKSHEET: *Test Comparison*

### Grade Log: Reading Comprehension

| (List names of each student.)<br>Student Name: | (List comprehension test grades before and after project.)<br>Grade: | |
| --- | --- | --- |
| | Pre-Project Test | Post-Project Test |
| | | |
| | | |
| | | |
| | | |
| | | |
| | | |
| | | |
| | | |
| | | |
| | | |
| | | |
| | | |
| | | |
| | | |
| | | |
| | | |
| | | |
| | | |
| | | |
| | | |
| | | |
| Average Grades for Class: | | |

Granted!

## WORKSHEET: *Report/Presentation Rubric*

NAME OF STUDENT:                                              DATE:

| Criteria | 4 | 3 | 2 | 1 | POINTS |
|---|---|---|---|---|---|
|  |  |  |  |  |  |
|  |  |  |  |  |  |
|  |  |  |  |  |  |
|  |  |  |  |  |  |
|  |  |  |  |  |  |
|  |  |  |  |  |  |
|  |  |  |  |  |  |
|  |  |  |  |  |  |

**TOTAL POINTS:**                              **Grade:**

| WORKSHEET: *Key Findings and Recommendations* | |
|---|---|
| KEY FINDINGS | RECOMMENDATIONS |
| | |
| | |
| | |
| | |
| | |
| | |
| | |
| | |
| | |
| | |
| | |
| | |
| | |
| | |
| | |
| | |
| | |
| | |
| | |
| | |
| | |
| | |
| | |
| | |
| | |
| | |
| | |
| | |
| | |

Granted!

## WORKSHEET: *Grant Evaluation Methodology*

| Date | Methodology | Results | Comments |
|------|-------------|---------|----------|
|      |             |         |          |
|      |             |         |          |
|      |             |         |          |
|      |             |         |          |
|      |             |         |          |
|      |             |         |          |
|      |             |         |          |
|      |             |         |          |
|      |             |         |          |
|      |             |         |          |
|      |             |         |          |
|      |             |         |          |
|      |             |         |          |
|      |             |         |          |
|      |             |         |          |
|      |             |         |          |
|      |             |         |          |
|      |             |         |          |
|      |             |         |          |
|      |             |         |          |
|      |             |         |          |
|      |             |         |          |
|      |             |         |          |
|      |             |         |          |
|      |             |         |          |
|      |             |         |          |
|      |             |         |          |
|      |             |         |          |
|      |             |         |          |
|      |             |         |          |
|      |             |         |          |
|      |             |         |          |
|      |             |         |          |
|      |             |         |          |
|      |             |         |          |
|      |             |         |          |
|      |             |         |          |
|      |             |         |          |

**TIMELINE**

| WORKSHEET: **Narrative Timeline:** *Sequence of Activities and Associated Timeframes* | |
|---|---|
| DATE: | ACTIVITY: |

TIMELINE

*Objective:*

| Activity | Do What? | By Whom? | When? | Challenges Expected |
|----------|----------|----------|-------|---------------------|
|          |          |          |       |                     |
|          |          |          |       |                     |
|          |          |          |       |                     |
|          |          |          |       |                     |
|          |          |          |       |                     |
|          |          |          |       |                     |
|          |          |          |       |                     |
|          |          |          |       |                     |
|          |          |          |       |                     |
|          |          |          |       |                     |

**TIMELINE**

## WORKSHEET: *Teacher Grant Timeline*

| Date(s) | Event | Actual Completion Date(s) | Comments |
|---------|-------|---------------------------|----------|
|  |  |  |  |
|  |  |  |  |
|  |  |  |  |
|  |  |  |  |
|  |  |  |  |
|  |  |  |  |
|  |  |  |  |
|  |  |  |  |
|  |  |  |  |
|  |  |  |  |
|  |  |  |  |
|  |  |  |  |
|  |  |  |  |
|  |  |  |  |
|  |  |  |  |
|  |  |  |  |
|  |  |  |  |
|  |  |  |  |
|  |  |  |  |
|  |  |  |  |
|  |  |  |  |
|  |  |  |  |
|  |  |  |  |
|  |  |  |  |

Granted!

WORKSHEET: *Chart Format Project Timeline*

Activity:

Dates:

[Your Name]
[School]
[Address]
[Date]

[Grant Entity Representative]
[Grant Entity]
[Address]

Dear _____:

Thank you for the generous award of a grant in the amount of $ _____ made by ___(Grant Entity)__ to ____(Your School)____ .

(Briefly summarize information about your school and the students impacted by the grant award, as well as the need to support education standards, etc.)

(Provide a short summary of the project that will be funded and how it will address this need.)

(If appropriate, you may include an invitation to the grant entity representative or others from the organization to visit your school and witness the project in action or invite them to a reception or similar event.)

Thank you again for your kind and generous support.

Sincerely,


[Your Name]
[Title]

(Photo)

(Photo Caption)
**High-res photos available.**

FOR IMMEDIATE RELEASE
Contact:
Your Name:
Your School:
Address:
Phone:
Email:
janedoe@nes.xyz.edu

(HEADLINE/ALL CAPS) _____

(Location)_____ – (Date)_____ -- (story)_____

_____

_____

_____

_____

_____

_____

_____

_____

_____

_____

_____

_____

_____

_____

_____

_____

– END –

**PUBLICITY & OUTREACH**

**NOTES:**

WHO WILL BE INVITED: _____

_____

TIME/PLACE: _____

_____

PERMISSION OF ADMINISTRATION: _____

_____

CONTACT WITH PARENT VOLUNTEER, ETC., REGARDING REFRESHMENTS, ETC. _____

_____

INVITATION FORM:

**You are invited to a**

_____
(the event)
**to honor**

_____
(students and/or their work)

**and** _____
(grant entity)

**regarding** _____
(the project)

Date: _____

Time: _____

Place: _____

RSVP: _____

**We hope to see you at** _____
(the event)

**made possible through the generosity of** _____ .
(the grant entity)

PUBLICITY & OUTREACH

Title of Grant:

Date of Funding:

**_Provide information about the students who participated in your funded project._**

Total number:

Minority students:

Grade levels/ages:

Total number on free lunch program:

Gender:  males                    ; females

**_Report your final budget.  Attach receipts to Final Report._**

Amount of funding originally approved          $

Amount expended                                        $

**_If the amount approved differs from the amount expended, explain why._**

| Budget Item | Proposed Budget | Actual Amount Expended |
|---|---|---|
|  |  |  |
|  |  |  |
|  |  |  |

• Describe funded project, including expected outcomes, as stated in your grant application.

• Describe the actual outcomes of the project.

• Summarize the methods you used to evaluate your project and the results.

• Provide the strengths and weaknesses of your project, including your analysis of items purchased through the grant.

• What were the most important things your students learned through the project?

• Provide information about any services funded through the grant such as work of an artist-in-residence.

Name                                             Contact information

Description of his/her services, including fees:

Description of how those services assisted in meeting the goals of the project:

• Submit photographs of activities funded by the grant for publication by grant entity.

• Describe your dissemination of information about the project, including findings, results and outcomes.

• State your recommendations for future projects or activities using grant materials or data.

 Granted!

**FINAL REPORT**

School or Organization Name: _____

School or Organization Street Address: _____

City: _____  ZIP Code: _____

County: _____

Phone # of School or Organization: _____

School District Name: _____

Applicant Name and Title: _____

Applicant's E-mail address: _____

Total # of Students Impacted: _____  Grade(s) of Students: _____

Amount of Funding Received: $ _____

Date of project: _____

## ASSESSMENT:

Submit up to two typed pages describing the activities undertaken as part of the field trip.

Include:

- description of field trip goals and measurable objectives

- concepts learned, how they were incorporated into existing school curriculum and how student knowledge was assessed

- previsit onsite and/or post-visit activities

- *State Learning Standards* met or supported

- list of partners and/or community resources used

- how funds were expended

## INCLUDE AS ATTACHMENTS:

- all receipts documenting expenditures

- photographs of students involved in project

- student reports or other work involved in project

- completed parent releases regarding photos and students' work

Final Report Due Date: _____

Mail To: _____

Original and Copies: _____